GOAL SETTING

THE ULTIMATE GUIDE TO ACHIEVING LIFE-CHANGING GOALS

THIBAUT MEURISSE

© 2017 Thibaut Meurisse

All rights reserved. No portion of this book may be reproduced in any form without permission from the publisher, except as permitted by U.S. copyright law.

CONTENTS

What This Book is and Who It is For	v
Your Free Step-by-Step Workbook	vii
How to Use This Book	ix
Introduction	xi
1. Why Goal Setting Is Important	1
2. How to Set Exciting Goals	7
3. Setting SMARTEST Goals	27
4. Other Key Considerations	92
Conclusion	103
What do you think?	105
Bibliography	107
Other Books By The Authors:	111
About the Author	113
Untitled	115
Wake Up Call - Preview	117
Step-by-Step Workbook	125
1. Why Goal Setting is Important	127
2. How to Set Exciting Goals	129
3. Setting SMARTEST Goals	139
Notes	155

What This Book is and Who It is For

You'll find many books on goal setting out there. Unfortunately, many fail to incorporate all the elements required for effective goal setting. They may focus on the mechanics of goal setting or teach you how to be more productive, but few provide you with all the pieces of the puzzle needed to ensure you'll achieve goals that genuinely excite you.

In this book, you'll discover the **SMARTEST Goal Method**, a comprehensive goal setting technique that encompasses all aspects of goal setting and will enable you to set and achieve goals you're genuinely excited about.

The SMARTEST Goal Method covers:

- How to overcome your limitations and unleash the power of your subconscious mind so you can achieve more than you ever thought possible
- How to set inspiring goals that deeply reflect your values and purpose
- How to avoid the seven deadly mistakes most people do when setting goals
- How to craft a clever strategy to maximize your chances of achieving your goals, and
- How to elaborate a clear plan of action you can use right away to work on your goals, and much more.

To ensure you get the most out of this book, I've also created a step-by-step workbook to guide you through the goal setting process. My aim is to remove any barriers that could prevent you from taking concrete action toward your goals and ambitions.

You'll greatly benefit from this book if:

- You want a clear step-by-step method to help you achieve your goals and aspirations
- You want to set and achieve exciting goals that reflect who you really are
- You don't want to settle, and you want more out of life.

If you recognized yourself in one of the cases above, this book is the right one for you.

So, if you are ready for the ride, let's get started.

Your Free Step-By-Step Workbook

In addition to the workbook available at the end of this book, you can also get a electronic version of the workbook at the following URL:

http://whatispersonaldevelopment.org/goals

If you have any difficulties downloading the workbook contact me at:

thibaut.meurisse@gmail.com

and I will send it to you as soon as possible.

How to Use This Book

To get the most out of this book, it's essential you use the workbook available at the end of this book. It's also crucial you commit to doing the exercises. This book is full of valuable information, but remember: how much you get out of the book is highly dependent upon how committed you are to carrying out its recommendations. The ball is in your court!

Feel free to re-read this book as often as necessary. Repetition is the key to mastery! See this book as a guide you can use to achieve any of your future goals.

If you have any questions, please email me at

thibaut.meurisse@gmail.com

You can also follow me on Facebook at

https://www.facebook.com/whatispersonaldevelopment.org/

I'm looking forward to hearing from you soon,

Thibaut Meurisse

Founder of Whatispersonaldevelopment.org

My author page:

http://amazon.com/author/thibautmeurisse

INTRODUCTION

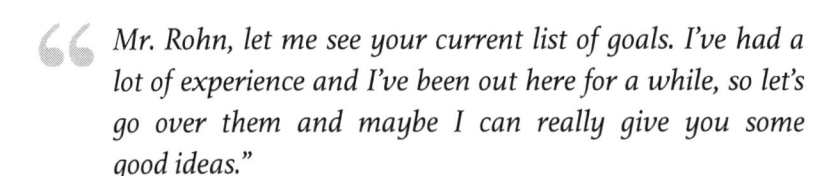

> *Mr. Rohn, let me see your current list of goals. I've had a lot of experience and I've been out here for a while, so let's go over them and maybe I can really give you some good ideas."*
>
> And I said, "I don't have a list."
>
> He said, "Well, if you don't have a list of your goals, I can guess your bank balance within a few hundred dollars."
>
> And he did.
>
> — Jim Rohn, The Jim Rohn Guide to Goal Setting.

Thank you for purchasing this book. In doing so, you have already shown your commitment to bettering your life by setting goals that truly excite you. You have joined those who have made the decision to take more control over their lives and give less power to circumstances. It's important to think about where you want to be, whether it's one month, one year, or one decade from now. Taking the time to identify your destination is the best way to make sure you're going into the right direction. It will also prevent you from pursuing goals that won't fulfill you.

Deciding to set goals is probably one of the most important decisions you can make, but most people don't set clear goals in their life. It's almost as though they believe they have no control over their life and, as such, they wander through life heavily influenced by the circumstances and people surrounding them. These individuals give their power to their environments instead of using it to create the lives they desire. By doing this, they achieve far less than if they took the time to plan their lives and set specific goals.

Keep in mind, however, that simply having goals is not enough. In fact, having goals that are unclear or out of alignment with what you want, can be almost as bad as having none at all. Unfortunately, many goal setters spend years in dogged pursuit of a particular goal, only to achieve it, and then realize it isn't what they genuinely wanted. This book will help you avoid this situation.

Setting specific goals is one of the best decisions I've made in my life, and the information within this book will give you an opportunity to do the same.

I first created a list of goals back in September 2014 while in the process of building my website. Looking back, I often wonder why I'd never done it before, and why I never learned about it in school. However, setting goals is essential when it comes to personal development..

I believe we all have the potential to accomplish great things in life. However, many of us never learned to tap into our intrinsic ability to self-motivate. We spend our childhoods studying to reach good grades and trying to 'conform', in an attempt to please our parents, teachers, or our peers. We then spend our adulthoods working for money and other external motivators, which are also called 'outside' or 'extrinsic' motivators.

Our tendency to rely upon external motivators is ironic considering how ineffective they are. Studies show that external motivators, such as money or praise, are less efficient than internal motivators like autonomy, mastery, or purpose. Autonomy is our desire to direct our own lives and have more freedom when working on a project. Mastery is our desire to get better, to master something just because we feel good about ourselves. Purpose is our desire to partake in something that is bigger than ourselves.

The carrot and stick approach is still in frequent use these days, but it's far from ideal, and not always successful in the longer term. In reality, internal motivation yields better results and provides a greater sense of fulfillment than external motivation does.

Fortunately, learning to set the right goals will help you tap into your intrinsic motivation and allow you to uncover your hidden potential.

This book will help you define your goals and the kind of life you want to create for yourself. It will help you set goals that inspire you, stir your soul, and make you want to jump out of bed every morning. Goal setting might seem intimidating at first, but trust me, the journey is more than worth it in the long run!

1
WHY GOAL SETTING IS IMPORTANT

> *People without goals are doomed to work forever for people who do have goals.*
>
> — BRIAN TRACY, AUTHOR AND MOTIVATIONAL SPEAKER.

Setting Goals Gives Direction to your Subconscious Mind

> *Your automatic creative mechanism is teleological. That is, it operates in terms of goals and end results. Once you give it a definite goal to achieve, you can depend upon its automatic guidance system to take you to that goal much better than "you" ever could by conscious thought. "You" supply the goal by thinking in terms of end results. Your automatic mechanism them supplies the means whereby.*
>
> — MAXWELL MALTZ, AUTHOR OF PSYCHO-CYBERNETICS.

Did you know your subconscious mind can help you achieve your goal? Setting goals gives you a direction in life, but vague goals, like making more money or being happy, won't lead to a fulfilling life.

Your unconscious mind is like a powerful machine, and understanding how it works is a big part of successful goal setting. Hypnotherapist Joseph Clough compares it to a GPS, whereas Maxwell Maltz, author of Psycho-Cybernetics, calls it a mechanical goal-seeking device. Consider it this way. If you give your GPS an address, it will do whatever it can to point you to your destination. The subconscious mind behaves similarly. Have you ever learned a new word only to find yourself hearing it everywhere you go? This is an example of your brain 'priming.' In other words, your subconscious mind is scanning your environment for all information relevant to the word, phrase, or details you've given it. This is why setting clear goals gives you a greater chance to accomplish them. This sends a strong signal to your subconscious mind, which allows it to unleash its focusing power and look for any opportunity to achieve the goal. I will talk more about the importance of setting specific goals later in this book.

Setting Goals Empowers You

> *If you don't design your own life plan, chances are you'll fall into someone else's plan. And guess what they have planned for you? Not much.*
>
> — JIM ROHN, AUTHOR AND MOTIVATIONAL SPEAKER.

Are you the one choosing your goals? Or are others choosing them for you? When you start setting your own goals in all major areas of your life, you stop giving your power away.

When you start setting goals in all major areas of your life—your finances, your relationships, your career, your personal life, and your health—you stop giving power away and start empowering yourself. You make a conscious choice to become the creator of your own life and begin to take responsibility for every aspect of your life.

Imagine the difference it would make in your life if you took the time to figure out your goals for the future. If you knew how much you wanted to earn in five years, how long you wanted to live, and where you'd like to be in twenty years, what would you do differently?

Setting Goals Increases Self-Esteem

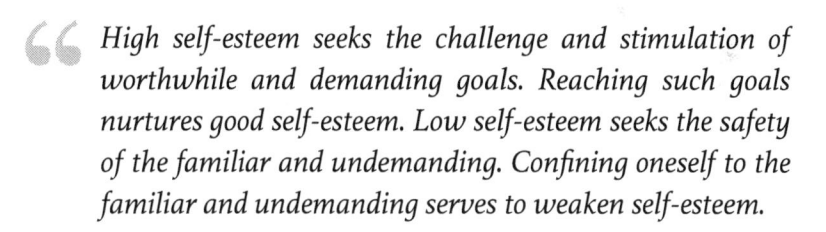

> *High self-esteem seeks the challenge and stimulation of worthwhile and demanding goals. Reaching such goals nurtures good self-esteem. Low self-esteem seeks the safety of the familiar and undemanding. Confining oneself to the familiar and undemanding serves to weaken self-esteem.*
>
> — NATHANIEL BRANDEN, AUTHOR OF THE SIX PILLARS OF SELF-ESTEEM.

Did you know you can increase your self-esteem by setting clear goals? It's worth mentioning that having clear goals and achieving them builds and reinforces our self-esteem. In fact, Nathaniel Branden (the author of "The Six Pillars of Self-Esteem") says part of our self-esteem comes from a 'disposition to experience ourselves as competent to cope with life's challenges.' With every goal we accomplish, we feel better equipped to deal with other goals and life challenges.

In his book, The Pursuit of Happiness, David G. Myers shows that high self-esteem is one of the best predictors of personal happiness. Consistently accomplishing the goals you set is one of the most efficient ways to build self-esteem.

Setting Goals Changes Your Reality

> *The value of goals is not in the future they describe, but the change in perception of reality they foster.*
>
> — David Allen, author of Getting Things Done.

Setting goals is a valuable process for its own sake, regardless of whether or not you'll achieve them. You're probably wondering why that's the case. Well, there are several reasons. Goal setting helps you think about your future, gives you an opportunity to reflect on your values, and helps you discover what really matters to you. It will bring clarity and allow you to see the bigger picture of your life. It doesn't get much more valuable than this, I'd say.

Setting goals will also allow you to reconstruct your reality and realize dreams you previously thought unattainable are in fact achievable. It all starts with identifying your true goals, no matter how ambitious they are. This starts the process of overcoming your limiting beliefs, which stem from past experiences and make it harder to get the life you want. You'll soon realize how restrictive limiting beliefs are and just how many of them result from repetitive messages received from family, friends, and the media.

Lastly, goal setting will give you the opportunity to assess your current situation and will lead you to close the gap between where you are and where you want to be.

Setting Goals is Good for your Health

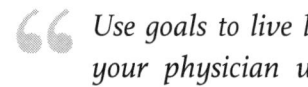
> *Use goals to live longer. No medicine in the world—and your physician will bear this out—is as powerful in bringing about life as is the desire to do something,*
>
> — DAVID J. SCHWARTZ, AUTHOR OF THE MAGIC OF THINKING BIG.

Dan Buettner, author of The Blue Zone: Lessons for Living Longer from the People Who've Lived the Longest, identified 'having a life purpose' as one of the nine characteristics shared by people who live to one hundred. Setting goals that really excite you is one of life's best medicines, and it will work wonders for your health. An alarming number of people die within a few years of retirement. One of the reasons for this, I believe, is they no longer have exciting goals to motivate them. This can be especially true for those who heavily identified with their job.

Still don't believe goals are good for your health? Check out the story of Miss D. from the book, The Magic of Thinking Big by David J. Schwartz:

> *Goals, intense goals, can keep a person alive when nothing else will. Mrs. D., the mother of a college friend of mine, contracted cancer when her son was only two. To darken matters, her husband had died only three months before her illness was diagnosed. Her physicians offered little hope. But Mrs. D. would not give up. She was determined to see her two-year-old son through college by operating a*

small retail store she inherited from her husband. She suffered numerous surgical operations. Each time the doctors would say, "Just a few more months." The cancer was never cured. But those "few more months" stretched into 20 years. She saw her son graduated from college. Six weeks later she was gone.

What about you? Have you found goals that will motivate you well into old age? If not, read on.

Action step

Clarify *why* you want to set goals and *what* you want to get out of this book (*Section I. 1. Your expectations*)

2

HOW TO SET EXCITING GOALS

1. How to Choose the Right Goals

The main characteristics of worthy goals

> *We can say that an individual is healthy to the extent that the basic principle of motivation is that of motivation by confidence (love of self, love of life); the degree of motivation by fear is the measure of underdeveloped self-esteem.*
>
> — NATHANIEL BRANDEN, AUTHOR OF THE SIX PILLARS OF SELF-ESTEEM.

I believe worthy goals have the following features:

1. They reflect your core values and are what you want, not what friends, family, or society wants from you.

2. They truly excite and energize you.
3. You enjoy the process that leads to them and not just the final outcome. "I'll be happy when…" types of goals are not goals worth pursuing. Why not be happy now?

To discern whether you're acting out of fear or love, you must closely examine your focus. **When you act out of love, your main focus is on giving. When you act out of fear, your main focus is on receiving something, be it money, approval, recognition, fame, or power.**

Acting out of love means you aren't trying to get people to like you, rather, you just want them to be happy. If you act out of love, the feeling of helping people, while doing what you love, will make you happy.

The desire to be famous, obtain money, or gain power can certainly motivate people to reach their goals, but people with such motivations are acting out of fear. They're trying to fill the emptiness within them through external recognition. I suggest, such goals are not truly worthy ones. In fact, they reflect a sense of insecurity and a lack of self-esteem, which is the very reason some seemingly successful people aren't happy. External things like money or fame never lead to true fulfillment. As Jim Carrey says, "I wish everyone could get rich and famous and have everything they ever dreamed of so they would know that's not the answer."

If your motives are external, ponder the following questions:

1. Do you feel as if you aren't good enough?
2. Are you trying to prove something to yourself or others?
3. What are you trying to achieve with your goal?

Acting out of love isn't easy and requires a great deal of personal development. You have to ask yourself frequently whether you're acting out of love or fear. You need to make a conscious effort to focus on helping others and personal fulfillment, rather than making money or gaining recognition.

Worthy vs. unworthy goals

An example of an unworthy goal is going into a field you have no interest in just because you think you can make a lot of money. This isn't a worthy goal. More often than not, you won't end up making much money if you don't like what you're doing. Identifying an unworthy goal is easier than you think. An unworthy goal won't reflect your values, nor will it excite you. The process of achieving it won't be enjoyable, and it won't involve giving to others, or acting out of love.

An example of a worthy goal would be going into a business you love, one that allows you to live by your deepest values. These values could be freedom, connection or contribution (see examples below). Either way, a worthy goal will stem from a sincere desire to make a difference in people's lives.

A worthy goal will reflect your values and excite you. The process of achieving it will be enjoyable, and it will involve both giving and acting out of love.

There's no guarantee you'll make a lot of money, but in the second case, you'll at least enjoy the process. Your goal will give you meaning. You're also more likely to persevere for a longer period due to your passion and genuine desire to contribute.

Below are some examples of values

Freedom is:

- Wanting to have a flexible schedule

- Wanting to work from home, and
- Wanting to travel regularly.

Connection is:

- Wanting to work in team most of the day, and
- Wanting to meet new people.

Contribution is:

- Wanting to feel you're making an impact on people's lives.

While we all aspire for freedom, connection and contribution, the degree will vary from one person to another as shown below:

- Freedom: some people may have a strong need to work on their own with a flexible schedule, while for other people the need for connecting with others or security, might be more important.
- Connection: an extrovert may have a stronger need for connection than an introvert.
- Contribution: Some people may need to feel the direct impact of their work on people's lives, while others may find greater pleasure in mastering their work independently of the impact they're making.

Questions to Consider:

Are you acting out of fear? If so, what does this tell about your self-esteem and the worthiness of your goal? What can you do about it?

The main pitfalls to avoid when setting goals

When properly done, setting goals empowers you. Even so, if you aren't careful, you might experience some obstacles. Now, I'm going to outline a few pitfalls so that you can avoid them. If you take these potential issues into consideration before setting goals, you'll be better equipped to face them successfully.

1. Being unaware of limiting factors

Our brain is wired to seek rewards and avoid pain, discomfort, and fear. It's not wired for change, so watch out for fear of failure. It can lead to self-sabotage if you don't keep it in check. You'll also have to identify any limiting beliefs or mental blocks that may hold you back.

Solution:

Become aware of, manage, and eradicate limiting beliefs. (I'll have more on that in the section "Transferring Your Goals to the Subconscious.")

2. Focusing excessively on your goal

This involves becoming so focused on your goal that you neglect other aspects of your life.

Solution: Be sure to reevaluate your goal on a regular basis and assess how it fits in your life as a whole.

3. Going too big

In an article entitled, *"The Hazards of Goal Pursuit,"* L.A. King and C.M. Burton argue that we should only use goals in the narrowest of circumstances. Their article states that,

> *The optimally striving individual ought to endeavor to achieve and approach goals that only slightly implicate the self; that are only moderately important, fairly easy, and moderately abstract; that do not conflict with each other, and that concern the accomplishment of something other than financial gain.*

Solution: Break a big goal into smaller goals to avoid taking on something that is too overwhelming.

4. Neglecting the now

Focusing excessively on future goals can cause you to dwell on what you don't have rather than what you do have, which fuels the individual's tendency to want more and more. It's important to feel good when living in the present moment and not just when you think about your desires. There must be a balance, so it's crucial to have goals that improve your present reality and accurately reflect your core values, rather than goals you can only enjoy in the future.

Solution: Using visualization every day to make you feel good about having that new house or car you desire is great, but isn't there more to life than this? Think about it and make sure you enjoy the present moment as well.

5. Getting too specific

Specific goals aren't bad, but they may keep you from seeing your overall progress. If you missed your weight loss goal by five pounds or accomplished something a week later than intended, for instance, you might believe the illusory notion you've failed. In reality, however, success and failure aren't so black and white. The primary function of goals is to ensure you live in alignment with your core values—they aren't supposed to make you beat yourself up.

Solution: Ensure your goals align with who you are and don't fixate on minor details. If you're unable to accomplish every aspect of your goal, congratulate yourself for the parts you did accomplish, and remember your 'why.' Missing some minor targets isn't the end of the world, and plenty of other doors will open as you continue the journey towards your major goal.

Also, make sure you focus on the process (what you do every day) and stay consistent. You have limited control over the outcome of your actions, but you have 100% control over the actions you take every day to move closer to your goal. We'll talk about the importance of having daily habits later in this book.

6. Having too many goals

Often, people fail to achieve their goals because they have too many of them. As a result, their effort and attention becomes diluted, preventing them from gaining tangible results with their goals.

Solution: Focus only on a limited number of goals at a time. Make a note of the other projects you'd like to work on and jot down ideas when necessary, but don't start working on them until you complete some of your current goals. You might want to schedule these goals for a later date.

7. Being a victim of the shiny object syndrome

Many people fail to achieve their goals because they keep jumping from one thing to another, never learning to stick to a goal long enough to accomplish it.

Solution: Avoid jumping from one course to another or one diet to the next. Instead, do your research, find something that works for you, and stick to it until you master the process. Eventually, you'll reach your goal. Set a few major goals and refocus on them whenever you feel overwhelmed or catch yourself doing too many unrelated things.

∼

Action step

Answer the questions in the workbook to shed light on some of the mistakes you make when setting goals. (*Section II. Setting Exciting goals - 1. How to choose the right goals - a. Setting worthy goals, and b. Avoiding Pitfalls.*)

∼

For more in-depth information regarding the process-focused approach, check out my advanced goal setting book, *The One Goal, Master the Art of Goal Setting, Win Your Inner Battles, and Achieve Exceptional Results.*

2. How to Set Inspiring Goals

> *The key to goal setting is for you to think on paper. Successful men and women think with a pen in their hands; unsuccessful people do not.*
>
> — BRIAN TRACY, AUTHOR AND MOTIVATIONAL SPEAKER.

If you want to set goals, you should first put them on paper. The act of writing them down using pen and paper will instantly make them more concrete in your mind. It's as though putting goals on paper moves the things you daydream about from the abstract world to the physical world. Daydreaming feels good in the moment, but it's just an illusion. Once you take the time to write down your goals, however, they start to become part of your reality.

A Simple Yet Powerful Goal Setting Exercise:

 Setting goals is the first step in turning the invisible into the visible.

— TONY ROBBINS, AUTHOR, ENTREPRENEUR AND LIFE COACH.

I'm going to share with you one of the most powerful exercise to set goals. Make sure you download the free workbook at http://whatispersonaldevelopment.org/goal-setting-workbook and follow the instructions (or use the workbook at the end of this book).

This exercise is very simple. All you have to do is **write down all the goals you would like to achieve if you were guaranteed to succeed no matter what.**

Focus on goals that really excite you, even if they sound totally crazy to others. What is it *you* really want? What *your* dream life would look like? What is *your* way to contribute to the world? Unleash your imagination!

I was talking to a friend recently and asked her if she had any dreams. She said no, but I had a feeling this wasn't true and asked again. I'm sure you can imagine my face when she suddenly said, "I want to change the world!"

"That's great! I want to change the world too," I replied. "The question is how are you going to do it? What is your unique way to change the world?"

She explained to me she thought her dream was too big. She said she would be happy if she could do something to change the world, even if it was something tiny. Like many other people, she wouldn't allow herself to dream big, but it's important to do so. You must allow yourself to dream big!

Whatever you do, **don't limit yourself in any way** while doing this exercise. Forget the excuses or limitations for a while and pretend you're playing a game. Make sure you're in a constructive state of mind. You can listen to your favorite song or whatever else elevates your mood. Take your time, do the exercise now, and ask yourself: What is it I want?

This process is crucial. It's unlikely you'll get much from this book if you skip it. So, go ahead and try it. Don't worry I'll wait.

All done? Great! How was it? How many inspiring goals did you come up with? How do they make you feel?

Now, here is the funny part. I want you to ask yourself this simple, yet powerful question: *How?* How are you going to achieve these big goals? If it helps, you can imagine you'll be beaten with birch twigs if you don't achieve them. Refrain from using limiting phrases such as 'I can't,' or 'It's impossible.' Ban these words and phrases from your vocabulary, and try to enjoy yourself, as you consider how you'll achieve what you want to accomplish. **Take at least ten minutes to brainstorm**, but you should only focus on your most important goal for now. You can think about the others later on.

Okay, now you've written down your goals and brainstormed how to achieve the most important one. How did this feel?

Next, I want you to ask yourself, "**What is one tiny step, if taken today, would get me closer to my goal?**" Once you've figured it out, take this tiny step today! It doesn't matter how small it is. It might entail sending a message to someone, buying a book, doing some Internet research, calling a friend, or going to a particular location. The particular action or activity isn't important—getting started is what counts.

I want you to remember this simple truth: **Every goal, regardless of its size, can be achieved through a succession of tiny steps taken every day.** The more you break your goal into manageable tasks, the easier it'll be to achieve. By taking small steps every day, you'll start building momentum and, therefore, continue to take action. Goals that once seemed impossible, will begin to appear achievable. You'll also avoid the pressure that comes when you try to deal with huge goals, which in turn, reduces the potential for self-sabotage. We'll discuss how to break down your goals in the section "Chunking down your goals."

Action step

Use the workbook to do the goal setting exercise mentioned above.

- Write down what you really want. (*Section II. - 2a. What do you really want?*)
- Write down how you're going to get there. (*Section II - 2b. How are you going to get there?*)
- Write down your very first step. (*Section II. - 2c. What is my first step?*)

3. How to Align Your Goal with Your Values

> *Neither pride nor self-esteem can be supported by the pursuit of secondhand values that do not reflect who we really are.*
>
> — NATHANIEL BRANDEN, AUTHOR OF THE SIX PILLARS OF SELF-ESTEEM.

It's imperative your goal is in line with your core values. If the goal you are pursuing is not in line with your core values and doesn't excite you, you are unlikely to achieve it. If you don't have a strong 'why' to support your goal, it will be hard to cope with the obstacles and failures you'll experience on your way to achieving it. You may even find it impossible to reach.

Identifying the values behind your goals

Understanding the deepest motivations behind your goal will make you feel good about what you wish to achieve, and will provide more reason to persevere when things become difficult.

So, take your biggest goal and ask yourself why it's important to you. What are all the values you attach to this particular goal? If your goal is to make a certain amount of money, figure out what values you attach to money.

In this section, I will share with you an exercise from hypnotherapist Joseph Clough that will help you not only identify the values you attached to your goals, but also supercharge them.

But, before we get started, as a warm-up exercise, I would like you to write your answers to the following questions using your workbook or a pen and a piece of paper:

- Why do you want to achieve this specific goal?
- What emotional benefit do you expect to gain by achieving it?

Don't overthink it, just write down the first thing that comes to mind. We'll be using your answers to complete the exercise.

Now, here is the exercise from hypnotherapist Joseph Clough:

1. Take a pen and a piece of paper and write down one specific goal you want to accomplish. I recommend you use the goal you've selected during the previous exercise.
2. Write down what values you'll get from achieving this particular goal
3. For each value go deeper by asking yourself why it's important to you (see example below).

To give you a specific example, here's a look at what I wrote when I applied this exercise to my most important goal (which is having a successful blog that generates 100,000 page views per month). I asked myself what achieving this goal would give me, and I discovered it would provide:

Fulfillment as a result of helping people

- Happiness

- Enhanced Self-Esteem

- Stronger sense of purpose

A passive income

- More freedom:

- Self-employment/independence
- An end to my daily commute
- The means of doing what I love
- The means to decide my own schedule

- Extra time to:

- Write more books and articles
- Study coaching, hypnosis or psychology
- Improve my public speaking skills
- Start new, exciting projects

- Better health:

- The ability to take a rest when I need to, and
- Less stress as a result of loving what I do.

This is just one example, of course, and you should fill in the exercise with whatever applies to you. The point is to go deeper and deeper into the benefits that your most important goals will bring you to create a stronger "why". **You can make any goal more meaningful by taking the time to think about the ways in which it will impact your life.** Go beyond the superficial. Think about how the goal will impact your health, mood, self-esteem, relationships, career, and any other important aspects of your life.

Now it's your turn! What is exciting about your goal? What benefits will you get from achieving it? Complete this exercise on the downloadable workbook (3a. What would achieving my goal get me?) and make your goal as exciting and inspiring as you can.

Action step

Use the workbook to write down what you'd get from achieving your goal. (*Section II. 3a. What would achieving my goal get me?*)

∼

4. How to Align Your Goal with Your Life Purpose

Life purpose vs. ideal goal

Now you know your most important goal, you should ask yourself, "What is the value of this goal?" **Remember, a goal is only valuable when the meaning we give it provides us with fulfillment.** Your goal is only one of several ways you can achieve the sense of fulfillment you're looking for, and it's important not to confuse your goal with your life purpose.

For instance, my life purpose is to, "Improve myself every day in order to live up to my full potential, and help others realize their true potential, so they can live happier, more fulfilling lives."

For me, realizing my life purpose was transformative. I was shy and passive most of my life, but eventually realized I wouldn't achieve my goals unless I started taking action. Without changing, I would reach my deathbed full of regret for not living the life I was supposed to, and for not having had the impact upon society I should have done. I didn't want such an ending, so I embarked on a journey of personal development that allowed me to come progressively out of my shell. I discovered I wanted to study, learn, evolve, and improve myself for the rest of my life. If I could work on myself, become more confident, and take more action, I could help others do the same. The main reason I've been able to start a blog, write a number of books, and shoot videos, is because these things are in sync with my values, and with what I want to get out of life. If it didn't motivate me, I wouldn't have the courage to follow through, leave my comfort zone, and keep moving forward despite challenges. Having a life purpose is without a doubt what motivated me to take action.

The idea of unleashing potential is also important to me because of the people I've watched miss out on their dreams. I have relatives who could have achieved much more in life, had they been able to overcome their lack of confidence, fear of failure, or limiting beliefs. Furthermore, I feel most people greatly underestimate their potential to accomplish great things in their lives.

My ultimate goal stems from my life purpose and has three parts. I want to become one of the best personal development experts, run a successful blog and write books that help people unleash their true potential. I could easily be overwhelmed by such an ambitious goal. However, this goal is *not* my life purpose. **If what I'm doing is in line with my life purpose, I will be satisfied even if I fail to achieve that goal.** I will feel fulfilled as long as I have a career that allows me to evolve and help others grow and maximize their potential. There is more than one way to do this, such as coaching or teaching, which may or may not involve achieving my ultimate goal.

Identifying the values behind a specific goal as we did in the previous exercise, opens us up to new possibilities and gives us more flexibility to adapt our goals to ensure they reflect our values. My goal of reaching at least 100,000 page views per month has no meaning in itself, the freedom and sense of accomplishment it will give me is what's important. Reaching 50,000 page views per month might generate enough passive income to allow me to live from my passion, while touching enough people's lives to provide the sense of contribution I seek.

Or perhaps having a few thousand loyal subscribers would generate the same results.

Setting an ambitious goal is still beneficial, however. In my specific case, it motivates me to do more and to give as much as I can to my readers. Setting your own ambitious goal can have a similarly motivational effect on you.

Identifying your life purpose

Knowing your core values and having a strong life purpose are vital components of having a life that is truly fulfilling. Unfortunately, many people will spend their entire lives pursuing worthless goals because they have no sense of purpose. **Most people lack a sense of purpose because they don't know themselves.** These individuals have been trying so hard to meet the expectations of their friends, parents, and societal expectations they haven't learned to listen to themselves. It's difficult to discover your life purpose if you don't know your core values, which is why it's crucial to spend time getting to know yourself.

To reach the essence of who you are, you must take steps to eliminate your limiting beliefs and deconstruct the false reality that was created by your environment. Otherwise, you risk coming up with a life purpose that's mostly the product of external influences. Remember this, because you cannot accept anything out of alignment with your belief system, the life purpose you discover will always be a reflection of your own subjective reality. As such, it may be necessary to change your belief system before you can find your true purpose. Discovering your life purpose will allow you to unleash your potential and, by doing so, work won't feel like work anymore. As Confucius said, "Choose a job you love, and you will never have to work a day in your life."

Finding your life purpose might take some time. Be patient and learn to listen to your emotions. Identify what you are passionate about and see what this says about your values. **Once you've** discovered your true passion, commit to it, take action, and persevere.** When you do this, it will be very hard for people or circumstances to stop you!

The characteristics of a great life purpose

To further help you, let me give you the main characteristics of a great life purpose. A great life purpose should be:

1. **Timeless:** If you could use a time travel machine and go back in time or travel to the future, your life purpose would remain the same.
2. **Universal:** If you were born in a different part of the world your purpose would still be the same.
3. **Inspiring:** Your life purpose should be truly inspiring, allowing you to unleash your full potential, and enabling you to experience a real sense of fulfillment. When your purpose resonates within you, what you're doing doesn't feel like work.
4. **Transcendent:** Your life purpose should help you transcend your fears and insecurities. Most people seek to gain recognition or feel accepted by society. These are fear-based motivators. **A genuine life purpose should encourage you to act from a place of love, not fear.**

3 practical exercises to discover your life purpose

Now, let me give you some exercises to help you discover your life purpose.

Exercise 1:

Take the most important goal you identified during the goal setting exercise. This goal in itself could certainly be a way for you to express your life purpose. What are the values behind this goal?

Take some time to think about these values and try to connect them with a possible life purpose.

Exercise 2:

Ask yourself the following questions:

- If I had all the money and time in the world what would I do? - This question removes any sense of limitation and allows you to go wild.
- What do I love so much that I'd pay to do it? - This question helps you find out what you really love to do.
- How can I get paid to do what I love to do? - This question allows you to brainstorm potential ideas to help you design your dream career.
- Who do I envy? - When you envy other people, it's usually because they have something you want. As such, this question can help you discover what you really want to do.

Exercise 3:

Take a pen and a piece of paper and answer the following question: "What is my life purpose?" Don't overthink it, just write whatever comes to mind. Keep doing it until the sentence you write makes you cry.

This exercise is originally from Steve Pavlina's article, *How to Discover Your Life Purpose in About 20 Minutes*. For more information type, "How to discover your life purpose in about 20 minutes" in your favorite search engine.

∼

Action step

Complete some or all of the three exercises above using the workbook. (*Section II. 4a. Discovering my life purpose.*)

∼

3

SETTING SMARTEST GOALS

> *As long as you are alive, you'll either live to accomplish your own goals and dreams, or you'll be used as a resource to accomplish someone else's goals and dreams.*
>
> — GRANT CARDONE, AUTHOR AND MOTIVATIONAL SPEAKER

Now we've discussed how to set exciting goals that are in line with your values and life purpose, we're going to delve more deeply into the goal setting process. In this section, you'll learn how to set goals effectively using the **SMARTEST Goals Method.**

More specifically, you'll learn:

- How to set specific, measurable goals you'll actually achieve
- How to prepare yourself mentally, develop great perseverance, and achieve your goals

- How to strategize effectively to maximize your chances of reaching your goals
- How to chunk down your goals and schedule tasks effectively, and
- How to reprogram your mind to overcome limiting beliefs.

SMART Goals Method

You may have heard about SMART goals before, but it's worth reviewing what they are before we delve into the SMARTEST Goals Method.

SMART stands for:

- **Specific**: you know exactly what your goal is.
- **Measurable**: you can measure and track your goal.
- **Achievable**: your goal is realistic (i.e. you believe you can achieve it).
- **Relevant**: your goal is relevant to you (i.e. it is exciting and meaningful).
- **Time-bound**: you have a clear deadline for your goal.

SMART goals are effective, but, when it comes to setting and achieving goals, it's just one part of a bigger picture. The SMART method focuses solely on technical issues, and overlooks psychological issues such as your belief system, your mental preparation, and the overall strategic planning needed to achieve your goal. For this reason, I recommend using the **SMARTEST Goals Method** instead.

SMARTEST goals build upon SMART goals and offer a more comprehensive approach to goal setting.

The SMARTEST Goals Method

SMARTEST stands for:

- **S**pecific: What exactly do you want? What are you trying to achieve?
- **M**easurable: Can you assess the progress towards your goal easily? How will you know whether you've achieved it?
- **A**chievable: Is it achievable? Is the timeframe realistic? Can you put in the effort required despite other responsibilities?
- **R**elevant: Is it in line with your values? Is it exciting you?
- **T**ime-bound: Do you have a clear deadline for your goals?
- **E**motionally Sustainable: Are you mentally prepared for the obstacles you'll encounter during the journey towards your goal? Learning to persevere is vital to your success!
- **S**trategized: Do you know exactly how you're going to reach your goals? Do you know the key factors for your success? What skills must you master? How must you prioritize your actions to reach your goal?
- **T**ransfer goals to the Subconscious: Most of us have limiting beliefs, many of which may be subconscious. You must take eliminating these limiting beliefs **very** seriously. Otherwise, they might prevent you reaching your goal.

From now on, we'll set goals that follow the **SMARTEST Goals Method**. We won't mention the "R" (relevant), which refers to the "why" behind your goals. We already covered this in the first part of this book when we addressed your core values and life purpose. We'll cover the following:

- Making your goal specific (S)

- Having measurable goals (M)
- Setting goals that are achievable (A)
- *(Setting exciting, relevant goals - covered in part I (R)*
- Having a clear deadline (T)
- Having an emotionally sustainable goal (E)
- Strategizing your goal (S)
- Transferring your goal to the subconscious (T)

1. Making Your Goal Specific (S)

> *Know what you want. Clarity is power. And vague goals promote vague results.*
>
> — ROBIN SHARMA, AUTHOR AND LEADERSHIP SPEAKER.

By now, you should have a clear idea of the values behind your goal. The next step is to ensure your goal is as specific as possible. Your mind likes clarity, and having clear goals will drive you to take action. It's almost impossible to move forward with vague goals.

An example of clarity's power

For a deeper understanding of clarity's importance, let's do a quick exercise from the book *Made to Stick* by Chip and Dan Heath:

Take fifteen seconds to list as many white things as you can. How many things could you think of?

Now take fifteen seconds to list as many white things in your refrigerator as you can.

Action step

Use the workbook to do the exercise now. I'll wait for you and give you my own answers. (*Section III. 1a. The power of clarity.*)

My answers:

- For the first question, I came up with things like Apple computers and snow.
- For the second question, some of the things I came up with were eggs, tofu, salad dressing, and the fridge itself. Most people can list as many white things in their refrigerators as they can in the entire world!

This exercise goes to show that specific goals allow you to tap into the focusing power of your mind. Vague goals do not, so your mind won't be able to support you in achieving them.

Clarifying your goals

The truth is most people never learn to clarify their goals. Last December, I asked a friend if he had any goals for the New Year, to which he replied he wanted to study Japanese and eat more healthily. Unfortunately, those are not goals. They're merely imprecise ideas.

The clearer version of my friend's goal to study Japanese might be something along the lines of, "I will study Japanese 30 minutes every day right after I take a shower." He would then need to decide what exactly he's aiming for and in what timeframe. He might decide he wants to be able to have a conversation in Japanese, write 500 Kanji (Chinese characters), or read a certain book in Japanese by the end of the year.

The goal to eat healthier food is as vague as the goal to study Japanese, but you could clarify it in the following ways:

1. I will eat at least five servings of vegetables every day.
2. I will refrain from eating sugar on Mondays and Thursdays except for fruit.
3. I will change from white to brown rice.

As you can see, it's much easier to act on your goals when you have a concrete plan and put it in writing. You'll know when you stray from the plan, and you can assess your progress more easily. Your goals will also be more tangible and easier to visualize, which sends a powerful signal to your mind regarding where its focus should be.

The bottom line is this: The more you clarify your goal, the more likely you are to achieve it.

Key Lessons:

Your goal should be specific. You should know exactly what you want to achieve and what you need to do to accomplish it.

∽

Action step

Make your goal as specific as possible using the workbook. (*Section III. 1b. Clarifying your goal.*)

∽

2. Having measurable goals (M)

> *What gets measured, gets done.*
>
> — Peter Drucker, management consultant and author.

It's essential your goal be measurable. Otherwise, how will you keep track of your progress and adjust your efforts and strategies over time? And how will you know whether you've achieved it?

Some goals are easier to measure than others. For instance, "I'll earn $5,000 per month by the end of the year" is pretty straightforward. Either you're making $5,000 or you aren't. This would be the same for the weight you want to lose, or the pounds of muscle you want to gain.

In other situations, making your goal measurable might be quite challenging. Our previous example, "I want to learn Japanese", would be one of these scenarios. With goals that can't be easily quantified, we must come up with our own qualitative criteria to measure our progress. For instance, "Having a conversation around travel with my Japanese friend," could be measured to a certain degree. Either you can talk about travel in Japanese or you can't. However, it's still insufficient and would have to be further defined by establishing specific criteria. Think of the way judges evaluate speeches or sports performances. They have a notation system. It's not perfect, but it ensures a certain degree of fairness when assessing participants performances. A similar system is necessary for qualitative goals.

What about you? How will you measure your goal?

Setting your KPIs

Key Performance Indicators (KPI) are indicators used in business to measure the performance of companies, departments within companies, and even employees. KPIs can also be applied to personal goals. If you want to write a book, the number of pages you write per day, week or month would be a KPI. Another KPI could be how many words you write per hour. If you can only dedicate 30 minutes per day, 5 days a week to your goal, and plan to write a 200-page book in a year, you would need to write an average of 0.77 pages per day (200 / 5 x 52 weeks = 0.77 pages/day). One page is about 250 words, so you'd need to write an average of 192.5 words per day. Assuming 30 minutes of work per day, that would require writing less than 400 words per hour which is more than doable. Of course, you would need to factor in time for editing, research, and other activities as well.

Setting a clear KPI of 200 words per day and assessing your progress on a weekly and monthly basis would ensure you stay on track with your goal and achieve it within the set timeframe.

For the goal of studying Japanese, it could be the amount of time spent studying each day, or counting the increase in your vocabulary.

What KPIs could you set to help you achieve your goals?

Key Lessons:

You don't know whether you've achieved a goal until you have a specific way to measure it. Make sure:

- Your goal can be measured (so you should know whether you've achieved it or not)

- It can be measured using quality measurements that are effective (for a non-quantifiable goal)
- You use KPIs to track the progress you make on your goal (words written per day, for instance)

Action step

- Use the workbook to write down your goal while ensuring that it's measurable. (*Section III. 2a. Having measurable goals.*)
- Set KPIs for your goal. (*Section III. 2b. Setting your own KPIs.*)

3. Setting Goals That are Achievable (A)

Setting a realistic goal

> *There are no unrealistic goals, only unrealistic timeframes.*
>
> — JACK CANFIELD, MOTIVATIONAL SPEAKER AND CO-AUTHOR OF THE CHICKEN SOUP FOR THE SOUL SERIES.

Gauging the feasibility of your goals can be tricky. When trying to discern whether your goal is realistic, it's best to use your feelings. Does it feel like you're struggling? Are you overwhelmed and frequently doubting your ability to achieve your goal? If so, you need to break the goal down into smaller steps.

Be honest with yourself regarding how you feel about your goal. If it doesn't sound realistic under the current timeframe, change the timeframe or break the goal down into smaller steps until you feel confident you can achieve it. Attaining your goal should be challenging enough to push you out of your comfort zone, but it shouldn't encourage self-sabotage or make you feel overwhelmed and discouraged.

For instance, as I mentioned before, my ultimate goal is to increase the traffic of my website at least 100,000 page views per month. I could easily become discouraged and ultimately give up if this was my only milestone. If I start small and focus on reaching 20,000 views per month over the course of 6 months, however, it sounds much more realistic.

If you don't believe that you can achieve a goal because it feels too big, you don't deserve it, or for any other reason, you'll struggle to achieve it. Worse yet, you're likely to engage in self-sabotage. This risk applies to conscious doubts as well as subconscious ones (there'll be more on that in the section "Emotionally Sustainable").

∽

Action step

Assess how realistic your goal is by referring to the workbook. (*Section III. 3a. Setting realistic goals.*)

∽

Chunking down your goal

As Henry Ford said, "Nothing is particularly hard if you break it down into small jobs." Your current goal may be extremely ambitious. But no matter how big it may be, you can always break it down into small, manageable tasks. It could be writing a page per day of the book you've always wanted to write. Or it could be studying fifteen minutes per day for the Japanese language test you want to take in a year or two. Or perhaps it's writing down all the tasks you need to complete for your side project and creating monthly, weekly, and daily objectives. As you can see, breaking your goals into 'bite size' chunks can be very beneficial. It allows you to avoid feeling overwhelmed and enables you to monitor your progress effectively.

Breaking down your goals and achieving small ones each and every day will also allow you to build momentum and gain confidence in your ability to achieve bigger goals. This, in turn, will boost your self-esteem.

Now, let's come back to the previous goal, "I want to study Japanese". Let's assume the main objective is to have a conversation in Japanese. For example's sake, we could further break it down as follows:

- By January 30th, I'll finish the first 10 lessons of my Japanese manual.
- By February 15th, I'll have a conversation in Japanese using the grammatical form and vocabulary introduced in the first 10 lessons of the manual.
- By February 28th, I'll complete all the lessons in my Japanese manual.
- By March 15th, I'll have a conversation with my Japanese friend in which I'll use all the grammatical points I've studied in the manual.
- By March 31st, I'll finish reading the Japanese book I bought the other day and verbally summarize it in

Japanese. I'll also prepare for some of the questions my friend may ask.
- By May 31st, I'll have a conversation with my Japanese friend about my experiences traveling in Asia.

These could be the main milestones for your goal of studying Japanese. Then, you would create weekly and daily goals. Maybe you would record yourself weekly using the grammatical form you've just learned. Or perhaps you would join a Japanese conversation group and make a conscious effort to apply what you learn in real life situations. These are just examples, of course, but you get the idea.

The bottom line is the more you can chunk down your goal and make your tasks manageable, the more likely you'll be to achieve them. Breaking your goal(s) down into manageable chunks allows you to:

- Define clearly what needs to be done to achieve your goal
- Set small, manageable tasks for each day or week, which prevents you from feeling overwhelmed
- Boost your self-esteem as you set and achieve small goals one after the another, and
- Build more momentum as you work on your goal every day.

Action step

Use the workbook to break your goal into monthly, weekly, and daily goals. (*Section III. 3b. Chunking down your goal.*)

Going after big goals

> *Don't set your goals too low. If you don't need much, you won't become much.*
>
> — JIM ROHN, AUTHOR AND MOTIVATIONAL SPEAKER.

On one hand, it's good to consider the feasibility of your goal. On the other hand, you want your ultimate goal to be something you truly want. You may wonder how big your goal should be. The answer to this question is: As big as you want it to be!

Setting big goals changes your outlook and perception almost instantly. It forces you to change your view of reality in order to find ways to reach your goals. You can't accomplish big things by setting small goals any more than you can accomplish a goal you haven't set or defined. Don't waste your time working towards something you don't genuinely want just because you think it's the best you can manage. Instead, create a big vision that genuinely excites you.

You might ask, "But what if my real goal doesn't seem remotely realistic to me right now?" and that's a perfectly normal reaction. If you earn $20,000 a year and your goal is to earn $1,000,000, it's logical your goal might sound unrealistic to you. This is where breaking your goals down into small, manageable steps comes in again. After all, a big goal is nothing more than a succession of hundreds or thousands of small goals achieved at regular intervals. When we look at successful people, we tend to see their accomplishments as something that came in big leaps. In most cases, however, this is an illusion. In reality, success starts with small steps and small gains.

So, remember it's the small steps you take every day that determines whether you'll achieve your goals, not the huge, hypothetical steps you may or may not take in the future. Get into the habit of working on your goals every day. You might tell yourself you'll do more tomorrow, but you probably won't. Always assume what you are doing today is what you'll be doing every day from now on. Then, ask yourself whether continuing to do what you've done today will enable you to achieve your big goal in the future.

As a side note, I don't recommend focusing too heavily on financial goals, but if you do, I would like to share this amazing Jim Rohn quote with you: "After you become a millionaire, you can give all your money away because what's important is not the million dollars; what's important is the person you have become in the process of becoming a millionaire." The point is: Don't forget to enjoy the process of personal growth. Try to see the creation of wealth as the result of personal development instead of your ultimate goal.

Wanting to become the best

Maybe your goal is to become the best in your field. In my view, there's nothing wrong with having such an ambitious goal. We should try to achieve as much as we can, and most of us are accomplishing far less than the best version of ourselves could. When we continually achieve less than we're capable of achieving, it's often due to the tremendous influence our environment has upon us. As motivational speaker Jim Rohn said, "You are the average of the five people you spend the most time with." If the people in your life don't make much money, for instance, it will be difficult to imagine earning five times more than they do. If, on the other hand, you have friends or relatives who are successful entrepreneurs, you would have higher limits regarding how much money it's possible to earn. Your environment plays a critical role in shaping your reality.

Even so, your environment doesn't have to determine how successful you will be--the mindset and limiting beliefs it created do this, but only if you allow it to happen.

Luckily, you have the power to change things. We have access to all the knowledge in the world through the Internet, and books have never been cheaper or easier to obtain. Your surroundings might be negative, but you can create a positive environment by reading things that are inspirational and by using positive affirmations each day. Your limiting beliefs formed through repetition. Therefore, you can overcome them through repetition, too.

If you overcome the limiting factors you can create a more empowering environment and keep growing until you become the type of person who can achieve your ambitious goals.

For more on that, refer to the section "Creating the Right Mindset" of this book. For an in-depth discussion of the topic, you might like to refer to my book *The One Goal: Master the Art of Goal Setting, Winn Your Inner Battles, and Achieve Exceptional Results.*

A final word about ambitious goals

If you have a particularly huge goal that few people can achieve (such as being a Hollywood star, for instance) make sure you identify the real "reason" behind it. What needs are you trying to meet through the goal? Are you acting 'literally' out of fear or out of love?

Remember, your goal is here to support you. It should improve your present reality. It should motivate you and make you feel good now, not just when you achieve it. If you aren't enjoying the process of achieving your goal but think it's attainment will bring you joy, you're deluding yourself. Joy isn't something you should wait for; it's something you should experience every day. **Your goal should bring you joy right now.**

Also remember, if you have deep issues, like a pervasive sense of being unworthy, achieving more won't usually solve the issue. In reality, the desire to achieve more is often a symptom of intense feelings of worthlessness. Deep issues must be solved by looking inward rather than outward!

Wayne Dyer beautifully wrote, "I am a human being, not a human doing. Don't equate your self-worth with how well you do things in life. You aren't what you do. If you are what you do, then when you don't ... you aren't."

Key Lessons:

Setting realistic goals is important. You don't want to be discouraged because you set a goal that is totally out of reach. To avoid this, make sure you follow this advice:

- Gauge your emotions and see how you feel about your goal. Does it excite you? Do you believe you can achieve it?
- Chunk down your goal into small, manageable tasks you can work on each day or week.

For challenging goals:

- Condition your mind for success by designing a more empowering environment, (refer to "Creating the Right Mindset" for more information).

- Make sure the route to your ambitious goal is enjoyable right now and not just in a hypothetical future.

4. Having A Clear Deadline for Your Goal (T)

> *A goal is a dream with a deadline.*
>
> — Napoleon Hill, author of Think and Grow Rich.

Parkinson's Law states "works expand so as to fill the time available for its completion." Without a clear deadline, your productivity may suffer and your ability to achieve your goals may be severely jeopardized.

It is therefore important to give your goals clear deadlines. For instance, it's better to say you'll finish a task by December 31 at 5pm than it is to say you'll finish by the end of the month. With a measurable timeframe for your goals, your chances of success become much higher. I'm sure you'll agree, the previous example of studying Japanese illustrates this very well.

Make certain you set a clear deadline for your goal and commit to it. Break your goal into smaller tasks and set sub-deadlines. This way, you'll know whether you're on track for success. You'll also be able to adjust your efforts and revise your schedule whenever necessary.

Then, take your deadline seriously. Do your best to meet your sub-deadlines one after the other. This will help you build momentum, increase your self-esteem, and strengthen your belief in your ability to achieve your goal. Keep your deadline in mind as you progress towards your goal.

That said, don't beat yourself up if you fail to meet your deadline.

Don't overreact and make a huge deal out of it. You don't want to sabotage your efforts and give up on a goal that's meaningful to you just because you failed to meet a specific deadline. As long as you accomplish what you intended, failing to meet an arbitrary deadline isn't a major issue.

Remember, setting realistic goals with realistic deadlines takes time and requires experience, not to mention all the things that may go wrong along the way. In the next section, "Emotionally sustainable", we'll delve deeper into the pitfalls you must avoid when setting goals.

Nobody can be 100% consistent. Things will happen along the way that slow down your progress. That's why you want to remain flexible. For example, I initially intended for this to be a short book written within a correspondingly short amount of time. However, while working on it, I realized it would be better to create something more detailed. I wanted to provide readers with a more comprehensive method, and I knew this meant extending my deadline. (For more on flexibility refer to the section "Other Key Considerations.")

Finally, we must mention there's not much pressure to respect deadlines when it comes to personal development. It's not like work or school where you're constantly held accountable by others. If this lack of pressure is a problem for you, you may need to set up an accountability system. For more on accountability, refer to the last section "Other Key Considerations."

Key Lessons:

Having deadlines for your goals is important. A clear deadline will:

- Make your goal more concrete and increase your chances of reaching it
- Force you to focus on your goal and prevent you from overworking yourself, and
- Require an accountability system, or a high level of self-discipline to be effective—see "Accountability Partner & Mastermind Group" in the section "Other Key Considerations."

Action step

Write down your deadline using the workbook (*Section III. 4. Having a clear deadline for your goals*).

5. Having an Emotionally Sustainable Goal (E)

> *In the long run, people usually do achieve their goals if they persist, stay flexible, and don't give up. The biggest challenge for most people is persisting long enough to win the mental game.*
>
> — STEVE PAVLINA, PERSONAL DEVELOPMENT BLOGGER.

Many people give up on their goals as soon as they encounter their first massive setback. I believe this is mostly due to a lack of mental readiness, and I'm convinced it can be avoided with enough mental preparation.

In this section, we're going to cover the psychological aspects of goal setting. More specifically, we'll cover the importance of identifying obstacles and planning for the worst. We'll also discuss how you can reframe failure and overcome self-criticism to achieve your goal.

Identify obstacles

Many people fail to accomplish their goals because they don't take time to identify the obstacles they might encounter or create strategies to overcome them.

Encountering obstacles that could stop you from reaching your goal is inevitable. You must be prepared to overcome these challenges if they begin to stand in your way. And they will! Let's say your goal is to lose weight. The list below summarizes some of the obstacles you may encounter.

- Hunger
- Dinner with friends, because it's difficult to eat healthily when everyone else is eating tempting foods that aren't part of your diet.
- Starbucks, because you're used to going there on your way to work.
- Emotional eating, because you tend to eat a lot when stressed.
- Lack of support, because you're the only one dieting in your family.
- Temptation, because your fridge is full of unhealthy foods.
- A weak "why," because you know you should eat healthily but don't feel motivated enough to do so.

In any of these instances, it would be good to consider what triggers you, what encourages you to eat unhealthy food, and what you can do to work around it. You might empty your fridge of unhealthy foods, join a support group, or enlist your friends to help you stay on track when you're going out with them. If you've tried unsuccessfully to eat healthily or lose weight in the past, you should figure out why it didn't work for you and see what you can learn from your earlier mistakes. It's also advisable to figure out your underlying thoughts surrounding food. Perhaps you associate unhealthy foods or excessive eating and drinking with enjoyable activities such as going to the movies, hanging out with friends, or spending time with family. If so, it would be wise to adopt new beliefs that don't inextricably link these things.

Now it's your turn. What major obstacles are you likely to encounter, and how will you overcome them? Take some time now to write them down using the downloadable worksheet.

Action step

Refer to the workbook and make a list of all the obstacles you may encounter as you work towards your stated goal. (*Section III. 5a. Identifying the obstacles.*)

Imagining the worst

We tend to be overly optimistic when we set a goal. I strongly recommend you do the following exercise to offset this:

Think of all the obstacles you may encounter during the journey towards your goal. Now, try to imagine what the worst-case scenario would look like. Don't be realistic. Think of the unexpected and imagine what terrible things could happen. Go wild! Then ask yourself what you'd do if these situations were to actually happen.

How would you feel? What would your reaction be? If you go through this exercise and write them down as a memory aid, you'll feel mentally prepared to face any challenge, and any setbacks you experience won't be able to stop you.

When tough times arrive, use this exercise to remind yourself of what you said you'd be willing to go through to achieve your goal. It's an essential step as it gives you peace of mind, focus, and perseverance, which is something people often lack.

Action step

Refer to the workbook and write down some of the worst-case scenarios (*Section III. 5b. Imagining the worst*).

Inoculating yourself against failure

How important is your goal? What are you willing to do to accomplish it? What are you willing to give up?

Let me tell you something: no matter how talented you are, you will fail many times. That's the reality. If you really want to reach your goal, you have to accept this truth first.

Most of us are afraid of failure, but that's a big mistake. Failure is actually one of the most important things in life because it's a necessary step towards success. Part of the reason our minds are so powerful is they operate through a process of trial and error to help us reach our goals. Regardless of your goal, you'll probably make small but frequent adjustments without even realizing it.

Failure is just a sign your actions and objectives have become too misaligned, and it's time to do something about it. You should see failure as your brain's way of telling you you're going in the wrong direction. It's just a sign you need to make some major adjustments to realign your actions with your goal. Failure is the biggest learning opportunity you will ever encounter. Successful people embrace it, unsuccessful people don't.

It's impossible to separate success from failure. Failure is succeeding! That is, it's an integral part of the trial and error process we call success, and it's something you have to go through to reach your goal. Being successful means having a healthy relationship with failure. As long as you learn something from setbacks, you can never truly fail. When you fail (and, at times, you surly will), ask yourself the following question: "What can I learn from this to help me move forward? Remember, it doesn't matter if you fail. Failure is normal. What matters is how you react to it. Don't just make peace with failure; learn to use it to your advantage.

Below are some "failure" stories to inspire you:

- Renowned sculptor Auguste Rodin's father referred to him by saying he had an idiot for a son. Described as the "worst pupil" in school, Rodin failed in all three attempts to gain admittance to art school. His uncle called him "uneducable."
- An expert once said of Vince Lombardi that he "... possesses minimal football knowledge" and "lacks motivation."
- Beethoven was awkward in handling violins and preferred playing his own compositions over improving

his technique. His teacher labeled him "hopeless" as a composer.
- The parents of famous opera singer Enrico Caruso wanted him to be an engineer. Worse yet, his teacher felt he lacked a voice and sang poorly.
- Walt Disney was fired by a newspaper editor for a "lack of ideas". He also went bankrupt several times before building Disneyland.
- Thomas Edison's teachers said he was too stupid to learn anything.
- War and Peace author Leo Tolstoy flunked out of college. He was described as being, "…both unable and unwilling to learn."
- Alibaba founder Jack Ma failed primary school tests twice and middle school tests three times. He tried to get into college three times but failed in each attempt. He then applied for jobs but was rejected thirty times. When KFC came to his city, they hired twenty-three out of the twenty-four people who applied—Jack Ma wasn't hired. He applied to Harvard but was rejected ten times.

So-called failures aren't really failures until they give up. As Norman Vincent Peale, author of, The Power of Positive Thinking, said, "It's always too soon to quit."

Make sure you give serious thought to what you're willing to go through to achieve your goal. Doing so is key to your success. Ask yourself the following:

- What would make me give up?
- Am I ready to be ridiculed by my family or friends?
- Can I keep moving forward even if no one believes in me?
- What am I ready to give up in order to achieve my goal? Going out? Going on vacations? Hobbies? Parties?

∾

Action step

Answer the corresponding questions in the workbook. (*Section III. 5c. Inoculating yourself against failure.*)

∾

Reconnecting with your "why"

Last but not least, ask yourself why. Why is this goal so important to you? When nobody believes in you, when things are not going well, or when the sacrifices are overwhelming, what will make you persevere?

I encourage you to write down your 'whys' and go through them whenever things are tough. The more you focus on the 'why' of a goal, the more you'll be able to persevere.

It may help to refer to the "Identify the Values Behind your Goals" section of the book when figuring out your 'whys.'

My 'why':

- **Why #1: I will earn money doing what I love.** Being told what to do by others doesn't inspire me, but doing what I love allows me to tap into my intrinsic motivation consistently and to accomplish more. It also grants me independence and allows me to avoid crowded offices and other workspaces that don't mesh well with my introverted personality.
- **Why #2: It gives me the freedom to work whenever and wherever I want.** I'm a French person living in Japan who writes books in English. Not surprisingly, I love to travel,

have a long list of countries that I'd like to experience. Earning passive income through my blog gives me the flexibility to travel and live in different countries.
- **Why #3: I will keep learning throughout my life.** I am easily bored and usually tire of repeating the same thing over and over. This frees me from being forced to do the same thing at the same company for the next thirty to forty years.
- **Why #4: I will help hundreds of thousands of people.** I can reach a lot of people through the Internet. It's both exciting and fulfilling to help others improve their lives.
- **Why #5: I will be happier.** I want to inspire people to grow, reach their potential, and find happiness. I must do this for myself if I want to help others do the same.

Action step

Use the workbook to write down the 'why' behind your goal. (*Section III. 5d. Reconnecting with your whys.*)

Dealing with self-Criticism the right way

I used to be very hard on myself but, more often than not, it wasn't in my best interest. This often caused me to give up on my goals too easily. You might worry you'll become lazy or complacent if you don't push yourself hard enough, but research shows having self-compassion works better than beating yourself up. I couldn't agree more with this. I've learned to be more compassionate towards myself in the past few months, and it has benefited in a number of ways. Self-criticism isn't good for us, it's related to self-sabotage and is usually the result of insufficient self-esteem.

According to recent studies, those who are more self-compassionate tend to perform better and persevere longer. Can you imagine how much more peace of mind and stability you would have if you were able to stop beating yourself up? The thing is, if you're being hard on yourself you're probably being hard on others as well. Don't get me wrong; I'm not saying you're being mean. You're probably very kind and compassionate with the people you know, but perhaps you're constantly misjudging those you don't know so well in the back of your mind. You might look around and think, "Why is this person eating unhealthily?" or, "Why is that person angry all the time?" or even, "Why is that person so mean?"

If this is you, don't feel bad. All you have to do is become aware of how much you judge others. If you find you are indeed judging people, start allowing them to be the way they are even if you don't like it. Tell yourself it's okay if they do this or that. Accept things as they are and assume these people have problems of their own and are doing the best they can. The more compassionate you are towards other, the more you'll be able to accept yourself for who you are: an imperfect human being among other imperfect human beings.

Interestingly, one of the characteristics of people with healthy self-esteem is the ability to judge their competence accurately. They don't beat themselves up for making mistakes or for failing, nor are they overconfident. In various studies, subjects with high self-esteem have been shown to persist much longer at a task than those with low self-esteem. If you want to know more about self-esteem, I highly encourage you to read *The Six Pillars of Self-Esteem* by Nathaniel Branden. I think it's one of the best books on the subject and contains this great quote: "Self-esteem is the reputation we acquire with ourselves."

To help you assess your level of self-esteem, there follows a brief summary of the six practices (or pillars) of self-esteem, as identified by Nathaniel Branden:

1. **Living consciously:** In Nathaniel Branden's words, "to live consciously means to seek to be aware of everything that bears on our actions, purposes, value, and goals—to the best of our ability, whatever that ability may be—and to behave in accordance with that which we see and know."
2. **Self-acceptance:** Is choosing to value yourself, to treat yourself with respect and stand up for your right to exist. Self-acceptance is the basis upon which self-esteem develops.
3. **Self-responsibility**: Is realizing no one is coming to save you and you are responsible for your life. It is accepting you are responsible for your choices and actions. You are responsible for how you use your time, and for your happiness. Because only *you* can change your life.
4. **Self-assertiveness:** Means, honoring my wants, needs, and values and seeking appropriate forms of their expression in reality.
5. **Living purposefully:** Is to use your powers to achieve the goals you have selected. In other words, it's your ability to set and achieve goals in every area of your life.
6. **Personal integrity:** Is behaving in a way that matches your ideals, convictions and belief. It's when you can look at yourself in the mirror and know you're doing the right thing.

So, what reputation do you have with yourself? Do you beat

yourself up regularly? How would your friends feel if you treated them the way you treat yourself?

Practice treating yourself the way you would treat an important houseguest. Be compassionate, and don't let negative self-talk discourage you.

Action step

Complete the corresponding exercise in the workbook. (*Section III. 5e. Dealing with self-criticism the right way.*)

Avoiding planning pitfalls

In the words of Bill Gates, "*Most people overestimate what they can do in one year and underestimate what they can do in ten years.*"

It's true we tend to be overly optimistic when making plans, especially short-term ones. That's why it's so common to see companies and government institutions going well over their budgets and missing deadlines on new projects. The more ambitious your goal is, the more likely you are to face unforeseeable difficulties. We're only human and certainly can't predict everything. You are likely to overestimate what you can do in one to two years, but you're also likely to underestimate what you can accomplish in five or ten. As such, I recommend you double the original timeframe for your goal.

In many cases, growth is not linear, and you might find you aren't moving forward as quickly as you expected in the first few months or even the first year. That's where most people quit, but don't give in to the urge to let go. Don't surrender. Hold on!

To illustrate the importance of patience and perseverance, motivational speaker Les Brown told the following story of the Chinese Bamboo:

> *The Chinese Bamboo tree takes five years to grow, and when they go through a process of growing it, they have to water and fertilize the ground where it is every day, and it doesn't break through the ground until the fifth year, but once it breaks through the ground within 5 weeks it grows ninety feet tall. The question is: does it grow ninety feet in five weeks or five years. The answer is obvious.*

Real estate investor and motivational speaker, Grant Cardone, recalls when he created his first business at twenty-nine years old. He thought he was prepared for challenges ahead, but he greatly underestimated the amount of effort and time needed to achieve his goal.

> *I assumed it would take three or four months to get back to that income level of the job I previously had. Well, it took me almost three years to get my business to provide me with the same amount of income of my previous job. That was twelve times longer than I had expected. And I almost quit three months into my new business venture. Not because of the money, but because of the amount of resistance and disappointment I was experiencing.*

I hope by now you understand the importance of preparing for the worse.

Action step

Use the workbook to adjust your deadline (*Section III. 5f. Avoiding planning pitfalls.*)

6. Strategizing Your Goal (S)

> *I find it fascinating that most people plan their vacations with better care than their lives. Perhaps that is because escape is easier than change.*
>
> — JIM ROHN, AUTHOR AND MOTIVATIONAL SPEAKER.

Achieving a goal means going from a point A (where you are now), to point B (where you want to be). There are billions of decisions we can make at any moment in our lives. There is always a way to find one of the many paths that will lead to your goal. Your job is to find it, and you need a clear strategy to do this!

In this section, we'll discuss the strategic aspect of goal setting and what you can do to maximize your chances of achieving your exciting goals. In the business world, companies spend a lot of time strategizing to reach their objectives, and this is exactly what you need to do as well.

Understanding the rules of success

Many people want to achieve something without knowing much about it. If you're serious about a goal, however, you should try to learn everything about it. You can start by purchasing a book or two written by experts in the area that interests you. You need to know the rules of the game if you want to win the match and achieve your goal. Figure out exactly what successful people are doing. How did they get there? What is their mindset? What are their daily habits? What challenges did they have to overcome? These are important questions to answer.

First and foremost, knowing this enables you to anticipate many of the difficulties you'll encounter. You'll be able to prepare mentally for those challenges and figure out ways to overcome them.

This knowledge will also help eliminate your limiting beliefs little by little. After all, the more examples you find of people who have accomplished what you wish to achieve, the more attainable your goal will appear.

Also, you'll be able to figure out why those who didn't reach the goal failed. You don't need to reinvent the wheel. **Spend as much time learning from people's failures as you do from their successes, and use the information/knowledge to reduce your learning curve.** You can't afford to overlook anything.

You should always be on the lookout for new information that will either help you to achieve your goal faster, or increase your chances of success. **Thorough planning is essential.**

Example:

How can I cut the learning curve when building my blog?

1. Read books written by people who have created high-traffic websites.
2. Join online communities of people who are creating successful websites.
3. Identify great websites from experts in blog creation.

Action step

Answer the questions in the corresponding section of the workbook. (*Section III. 6a. Understanding the rule of success.*)

Filling in the gap

Achieving a goal is always a matter of going from a point A to point B. Ask yourself what skills you must develop in order to reach your goal and figure out how to bridge the gap. **Identify the skills, if worked on daily, will help you the most to achieve your goal.**

Let's use my website as an example:

What skills do I need to build a successful blog?

1. Marketing skills.
2. The effective use of social media.
3. Finding and mastering the most efficient ways to create lasting traffic.
4. The ability to discern what my readers will find interesting and useful.
5. SEO (search engine optimization) skills.
6. Creating engaging, well-written, and inspiring articles.

What about you? What skills do you need to work on to reach your goal?

Questions to Consider:

1. What could possibly prevent me from succeeding?
2. Am I doing everything I need to do to reach my goal?
3. If I keep doing what I'm doing today/this week/this month, am I going to reach my goal?

∼

Action step

Use the workbook to write down the specific skill(s) you need to develop to achieve your goal. (*Section III. 6a1. Filling the gap.*)

∼

Using the 80/20 rule

When it comes to the work involved in reaching your goals, some things will have more impact than others. The 80/20 rule states that 20% of your efforts will account for 80% of your results. This ratio is only a rough indicator, but it's helpful nonetheless.

It's essential you identify the things which will have the most impact and focus most of your time on them. Make it a habit to start your morning with them. Review your progress on a regular basis, and don't use less important tasks to trick yourself into thinking you're working when you aren't.

If you doubt the effectiveness of focusing on a few key tasks, consider this excerpt from Gary Keller's book The One Thing. It illustrates the importance of focusing on a few key things rather than trying to do to many things at once.

> *As fast as we were growing, we were still not acknowledged by the top people in our industry. I challenged our group to brainstorm one hundred ways to*

turn this situation around. It took us all day to come up with the list. The next morning, we narrowed the list down to ten ideas, and from there we chose just one big idea. The one that we decided on was that I would write a book on how to become an elite performer in our industry. It worked. Eight years later that one book had not only become a national bestseller, but also had morphed into a series of books with total sales of over a million copies. In an industry of about a million people, one thing changed our image forever.

Finding your top 20% tasks

The first step to identifying the 20% of your tasks that generate 80% of your results is making a list of all the things you could do to achieve your goal. Try to come up with at least 20 different things. If you've already started to work on your goals, write down all the things you're doing in relation to them. Then come up with as many new ideas as possible.

The second step involves asking yourself the following question: If I could only do one thing on this list, which one would help me make the most progress toward my goal? Draw a circle around this task. Repeat the process until you come up with a list of three to five tasks. That's the top 20% tasks you need to focus on most.

Eliminating distractions

While some tasks produce tangible results, others are distractions in disguise. They include things like watching videos on YouTube, or reading books passively. For more awareness of these tasks, try writing them down. Consider them your 'not-to-do' list.

Action step

Use the workbook to write down your most important tasks and create your 'not-to-do list'. (*Section III. 6a2 Using the 80/20 rule.*)

~

Learning new skills with deliberate practice

For the most part, you can learn any skills you need to achieve your goals. These days, we live in a world where we're often one click away from the knowledge we need. Once you've identified the skills you need and the tasks you should focus on, it's time to master and complete them.

When you work on developing new skills, the way you practice is more important than the amount of time you spend practicing (quality beats quantity). Let's take someone who plays tennis for thirty years as an example. You'd think that playing for thirty years would make them a pro. If they've only played casually with friends, however, it's likely their skill level isn't much better than it was when they started. Research shows hard work and deliberate practice are more important than talent when it comes to achieving goals. **"I'm not talented enough" isn't a valid excuse.**

Deliberate practice involves meticulous training that focuses on the things/skills necessary to improve your performance. More often than not, it's mentally taxing, involves a lot a repetitive work, requires constant feedback, and isn't much fun. It's no surprise few people are willing to commit to it as intensely as those at the top of their fields do.

Sadly, this is why so many of us are stuck. Sure, we can enjoy playing a certain instrument, or we have fun playing a particular sport with our friends. This doesn't mean we're willing to practice the same thing thousands of times, run every morning, work out consistently, or anything else that's tough, demanding, and requires unswerving commitment. The reality is we're unwilling to put in the work required to go the next level. This is what keeps us stuck, not a lack of talent.

For a great example of intense, deliberate practice, let's take a look at Benjamin Franklin and how he became a great writer. Franklin took laborious steps to improve his writing style, vocabulary, and organizational skills. He mastered the first skill by making notes on articles from *Spectator*, a high-quality newspaper, which he would use to rewrite the articles a few days later. He would then compare his version to the original and modify it accordingly. He mastered the second skill by rewriting *Spectator* essays in verse and then in prose so he could compare his vocabulary to the vocabulary used in the original article. He mastered organization by writing summaries of every sentence in a particular article on separate sheets of paper. He would then wait a few weeks before challenging himself to write the article in the correct order and comparing his work to the original article.

Those three exercises required a lot of mental effort, focused on specific skills, involved long periods of repetition, and certainly weren't fun. What's impressive is Franklin practiced these exercises consistently while working full time in his brother's printing business. His methods would probably be effective today, but how many people would be willing to go through this kind of tedious, deliberate practice on a consistent basis? Very few.

The bottom line is this: **There's no skill you can't develop if you're firmly committed to your goal** and have the basic mental and physical capacities required. Some skills might be easy to develop while others may require hard work and deliberate practice; it all depends on the difficulty of your goal and what your starting point is.

Action step

Write down what you'll do to master the skills required to achieve your goal (*Section III. 6a4. Learning new skills with deliberate practice*).

Leveraging the power of daily habits

Speaking of the philosophy of Aristotle, historian William Durant, wrote: *"We are what we repeatedly do. Excellence, then, is not an act, but a habit."*

What you do on a daily basis is what will ultimately determine whether or not you'll be successful. Reaching your long-term goals depends on your daily habits. However, it's hard to think long-term in a fast-paced world whose products and advertisements encourage instant gratification. The fact remains, in the long run, adopting certain habits brings many benefits. Meditating for a few minutes a day, taking the time to express gratitude, or scheduling the upcoming day, for example, can create positive changes that significantly impact your life.

If running a marathon is your big goal, preparing a week before the event probably won't cut it. If exercise isn't something you're used to, you'll have to start small and gradually increase the intensity and duration of your training until you can handle the physical activity required to reach your goal.

Building momentum through daily action

There's nothing better than daily actions to build momentum. When you work on your goal every day, you'll build momentum that will stay with you as long as you remain consistent.

For instance, if you want to start a business, you could begin by checking out books on business creation. The next day, you could decide which books to buy. The day after that, you could seek the advice of someone you know who owns a business. By taking a succession of daily baby steps, you make the goal part of your reality. In doing so, your belief in your ability to succeed will increase. This will allow you to create a new, empowering belief system that will slowly but surely replace your old one.

Turning tasks into daily habits

Almost any task can become a daily habit. Breaking your goals down into daily habits helps build momentum and automate the achievement process. Unsurprisingly, this will vastly increase your chances of success.

If your goal is to write a book, you could write one page every day first thing in the morning. If you want to learn a language, your goal could be to study it for thirty minutes daily.

Starting small

To avoid attaching negative feelings to your new task, start small and do what feels comfortable. Choose a time commitment that you can stick with on a daily basis. Then, once it becomes automatic, you can gradually increase the time commitment as needed.

If you want to meditate for an hour a day, you could start with a minute a day if that's what feels manageable. If you want to run several miles a day, you should start with a few minutes each day. Once these practices become habit, you can spend more and more time on them. The amount of time you start with isn't important. **The point is to create a new habit and build momentum.**

Set "if ... then" triggers

Our day is a succession of small actions. Most of them, such as waking, showering, eating breakfast, brushing our teeth, and leaving the house, are automatic. We don't have to think about them to do them. You can take advantage of this by using the end of an action that is already automatic as a trigger for a new habit, which will help make the new habit automatic. "If ... then" triggers are a great way to do this, and can be seen in the following examples:

1. **If** I have just woken up, **then** I'll immediately drink a glass of water.
2. **If** I have just finished showering, **then** I'll immediately meditate.
3. **If** I just came home from work, **then** I'll immediately start working on my goal.

Setting triggers helps you save energy and prevent your willpower from depleting by creating habits that will become automatic after a while. Studies show that setting intentions can prevent willpower burnout.

For a detailed, step-by-step method on how to set long-lasting habits, check out my book *Habits That Stick, The Ultimate Guide to Building Powerful Habits that Stick Once and For All.*

Action step

Use the workbook to write down the three tasks you'll perform every day to reach your goal. (*Section III. 6a4. Leveraging the power of daily habits.*)

∼

Investing in your goals

You may be wondering whether you should invest in commercial software, books, and courses, or stick to free stuff online. If you have a lot of free time, the second option might work. You can find some amazing resources that way. However, they might be disorganized and finding the information you want is usually time-consuming.

Consider the following: If you search for the best possible way to learn the skill you need, you're going to find resources that throngs of people have purchased and used with success. Such programs must be worth as much if not more than their cost. Otherwise, no one would buy them.

Furthermore, time is money. Something that costs $100 might sound expensive until you ask yourself how much time you can save by purchasing it. You should also ask yourself how much you value an hour of your time. If the book or program allows you to save 10 hours of your time, for instance, you could invest this time in a part-time job. Let's assume you can find a part-time job that pays $10 an hour. If so, you'll earn $100, the cost of the program! Now, it doesn't seem that expensive.

Of course, the benefits of a particular program also extend to the value they create. If it's a popular product that helps a lot of people, it creates value. Value comes in many forms. You might make more money in the long run by using the program, but your gains might also be emotional. Perhaps it creates a sense of well-being or more satisfaction in life. It's up to you to decide upon a monetary value for non-monetary benefits.

Having an effective method you can follow step by step will also allow you to stay focused on your goal and avoid distractions. You don't want to spend all your time trying to figure out what does and doesn't work. It's best to find something you can trust from start to finish.

Last but not least, investing money gives you more incentive to take action. It shows your commitment to your goals. You're more likely to take action toward your goal if you hire a coach for $500 per month than if you found one offering pro bono services. Similarly, you'd be less likely to take action if you'd downloaded this e-book for free. Free isn't always in your best interest.

Remember, taking action is always the most important thing. As long as you put the advice of the coach, book, or product to use, your investment will be a good one.

Questions to consider:

1. How reliable is the program that I want to use?
2. How much time can I save by purchasing it, and how much do I value an hour of my time?
3. How much money will it allow me to make or save in the long run?
4. To what extent will it allow me to avoid distractions?
5. Does it provide other benefits (such as peace of mind or incentive to take action)?

If, after answering these questions, you feel that the cost is less than the time or money it will save, make the investment.

If you're short on cash and lack the education necessary to earn more money, it's crucial to invest in your education, even if it means substantial sacrifices. Otherwise, you'll be stuck where you are. There are boundless resources in today's world, and many of them are available at a very low cost. We lack neither resourcefulness nor options. Finding, investing in, and making full use of these resources is one of the keys to success.

Key Lessons:

To reach your goals, you must implement the right strategy in the following ways:

- **Understanding the rules of success:** Learn as much as you can from the successes and failures of people who have achieved what you want.
- **Filling in the gap:** Identify all the skills you must develop to go from where you are to where you want to be.
- **Leveraging the 80/20 Principle:** Prioritize like a champion. Focus on the 20% of tasks that produce 80% of your results. Get rid of the rest as much as you can.
- **Using deliberate practice:** You can learn any skill you need. Focus on your core skills and become so good at them that people take notice!
- **Forming daily habits:** Organize your daily tasks around your core skills and high-value tasks. Remain consistent and stick to your habits **each day.** Finally, automate your tasks by setting 'if ... then' triggers.
- **Investing in your goals:** Knowledge is the best investment you'll ever make. Make sure you invest your money in books and programs that can accelerate your success.

Scheduling for success

> *The things that get scheduled are the things that get done.*
> — ROBIN SHARMA, AUTHOR AND LEADERSHIP SPEAKER.

The more specific your plans are, the more likely you are to achieve your goal. Make a habit of planning your month at the start of each month, planning your week every Sunday morning, and planning your day before you go to bed. I always accomplish a lot more when I plan than when I don't. According to Brian Tracy, a leading expert in goal setting and time management, each minute you spend in planning saves as much as 10 minutes in execution. Make sure you don't skip this important component of the goal setting process!

Planning your month like a pro

A month is a big enough chunk of time for you to make concrete progress towards your goal. When you set monthly goals, you want to focus on a few tasks or projects you'd like to complete by the end of the month. I recommend focusing on three to six projects or tasks related to your goal. Ask yourself this: What tasks, if completed by the end of the month, will allow me to make the most progress toward my goal?

To create your monthly goals, set aside a few hours at the beginning of the month or the end of the previous month. Then do the following:

- Reflect on the progress you made during the month. Look at your previous goals and see whether you've achieved them or not. Here are two questions to ask yourself:

- What went well? What do I want to congratulate myself on?
- What could I have done better?
- What will I stop/start doing this month to improve my results?
- Review your long-term goals (e.g. the yearly ones) and your overall strategy to achieve them. Adjust your long-term goals if necessary.
- Write down the three to five projects or tasks you want to work on this month. These should be tasks that will allow you to make significant progress on your goal. Again, make sure your tasks follow the **SMARTEST Goal Method** and can be easily measured.

Create the habit of setting and reviewing goals every month. It will allow you to make great progress.

Final tip: Set a specific day and time each month that you stick to. Show up as you would for any formal meeting.

Planning your week like a pro

Identify three goals you want to accomplish during the week to get closer to your goal. These should be the best things you can do to move forward. To give a personal example, my goals could be as follows:

1. Completing a specific chapter of this book.
2. Writing one article and submitting it to major personal development websites.
3. Creating free content for my readers, which, at the moment, involves working on a chapter of another e-book.

I tend to be all over the place, so it helps to have a reminder of these goals whenever I need it. It keeps me from getting lost in irrelevant details and wasting time on things that don't help me accomplish anything.

Note that your three goals may not be the same every week—it all depends on the specifics regarding your particular goal. In my case, my main tasks would involve writing, but they could also involve promotion or marketing.

Make sure you set aside specific times to schedule the upcoming week. This way, you'll reach optimal results.

Planning your day like a pro

Before we have a detailed discussion on how to plan your day for maximum effectiveness, let me give you seven reasons why you should plan your day.

1. **To avoid distraction:** When you know exactly what you need to do, you prevent your brain coming up with reasons to procrastinate. Whenever you put yourself in a situation where you have to think about what to do next, you give your brain an opportunity to look for distractions. You might feel the sudden urge to check your emails, go on Facebook, or watch videos on YouTube. If you're not careful, you can easily waste hours on these things. Be aware your mind will almost always try to distract you, and be on the lookout for the ways in which this shows.
2. **To reflect on your strategy:** Planning gives you an opportunity to step back and look at the bigger picture. You can assess the efficiency of what you're doing and make sure you're focusing your energy on the things that are truly important.

3. **To limit the use of willpower:** Your willpower is a limited resource. Advance planning gives your subconscious a sense of direction. When this happens, you don't have to think much about what you need to do next. Your behavior becomes automated, and you don't need willpower to motivate yourself before each and every task.
4. **To build momentum:** Once you complete your first task in the morning, you feel a sense of accomplishment and relief, and this builds momentum for the rest of the day. This sense of momentum compels you to accomplish more throughout the day and helps create an effortless source of motivation.
5. **To increase self-esteem:** Many people fail to realize that self-esteem is linked to discipline. The more you discipline yourself to do what's needed, the better your self-esteem will be.
6. **To boost your productivity:** Completing your most important task first and focusing on one thing at a time will greatly increase your productivity.
7. **To reduce stress:** Planning ahead and knowing exactly what you'll have to do each day will bring you peace of mind. It will also decrease the amount of uncertainty you'll experience throughout your day. All you need is to complete the items on your to-do list one by one. It doesn't require much thinking and you won't be overwhelmed by all the things you need to do.

Now, let's see how you can plan your day to ensure it's a productive one.

Before going to bed make a list of three to five tasks that will help you move toward your goal. Now look at the list and ask yourself, "If I could accomplish only one task on this list, which one would have the most impact?"

Make a commitment to complete whichever task you choose first thing in the morning, and repeat the same process for the rest of the items on your day's list. Don't check your emails, read the newspaper, or watch television. Avoid anything that could distract you until you've finished at least two of the most important tasks.

Finally, whenever possible, set a specific time to plan your daily activities. **The more you plan the more efficient you'll be.**

Additional tip:

To further increase your productivity, you can visualize your day. Here is how to do it:

- After you plan your day, take at least five minutes to visualize it. See yourself accomplishing everything on your list. Picture your day going exactly as you want it to. Your subconscious mind will work with those images of success while you sleep.
- Repeat the process the next morning before you start your day. Setting your intention is an important part of staying on track and has been proven to increase willpower

Creating your list of goals

I highly recommend creating a yearly list of goals. It helps to divide your list into categories. When you categorize your goals, you decrease the chances of neglecting some parts of your life in favor of others. Better still, breaking long-term goals into annual ones makes them much easier to achieve. You can then break your goals down into monthly and weekly ones as discussed earlier.

The steps below can make creating your list easier and more efficient:

1. Use positive words and statements that show confidence in your ability to accomplish those goals. Use phrases such as 'I am,' 'I will easily,' or 'I will definitely,' when describing your intention.
2. Look over your list every morning.
3. Adjust your aims over time. You probably won't accomplish all your goals, and this is okay. Get rid of the goals that no longer resonate with you or can be postponed. Focus instead on the most important goals, the ones that will provide the greatest contribution to your fulfillment.

Remember: Don't stress out trying to achieve ever single goal you set. You won't achieve every single one, and this is perfectly normal!

You may have many different things you wish to achieve. However, it's important to focus on the ones that matter most and avoid trying to accomplish all of them at once. You will inevitably drop some goals over time, but you should always start by spending the majority of your time on the goals that excite you the most.

As previously mentioned, it's useful to apply the 80/20 rule for your goals. Focus on your most important goals. Focus is key! Ask yourself which goal you would choose if you could only accomplish one on the list. To prioritize your goals, repeat the process until you've gone through the entire list.

Key Lessons:

The better you plan, the more likely you are to achieve your goals. As stated earlier, failing to prepare is preparing to fail. So, make sure you do the following four things:

1. **Plan your month like a pro:** At the beginning of each

month, set aside some time to write down your monthly goals. Identify three to five core tasks you'd like to work on.
2. **Plan your week like a pro:** At the beginning of each week, identify three core tasks that will move you closer to your goals. Make sure you schedule them.
3. **Plan your day like a pro:** Write down three to five tasks you want to work on. It's best to do this in the morning or before bed the previous night. Then, rank all the tasks in order of importance and work on the most important one first. Go down the list until you complete all of your tasks.
4. **Create your list of yearly goals:** Write down your yearly goals and look at them often. Make sure you have goals in every important area of your life.

7. Transferring Your Goal to the Subconscious (T)

> *The war has begun and it's between you and you. There ain't nobody else in your way.*
>
> — ANONYMOUS.

When your subconscious mind lines up with your goals, you can achieve exceptional things. When it works against you, however, it often seems as though you're driving with the brakes on. When that's the case, you need more than a great strategy to achieve your goal.

In this section, we'll discuss how you can befriend your subconscious mind and overcome limiting beliefs. Then we'll see how you can reprogram your mind for success through daily conditioning. This will allow you to develop the necessary mindset to achieve your goals.

What are 'limiting beliefs'?

Limiting beliefs are the assumptions upon which we base our lives, which is why it's so important to know which ones are holding us back. Our reality is the result of our beliefs, and our worlds are limited by what we think is possible. These thoughts do not necessarily reflect the truth. What we believe we can do may be entirely different from what we can do in actuality. The first step to letting go of our limiting beliefs is to accept they are the subjective truth rather objective—they are not necessarily the actual truth.

Limiting beliefs can hold you back and create a reality that isn't the one you want. Your subconscious mind will always act in concert with your thoughts, even if you aren't aware of them. Beliefs are simply thoughts repeated so often and for so long your subconscious mind has accepted them as true. They are the reflection of your personal interpretation of the things your parents, friends, or the media have repeatedly told you. As such, the beliefs you hold may not be yours. It's entirely possible you've inherited them from your parents, who possibly inherited them from their own parents. Or, they might be the result of negative experiences in your past. Fortunately, there's no rule that says you must stick with a particular belief, especially the ones you haven't consciously chosen. It's vital to understand you are not your mind, your thoughts, or your limiting beliefs. You are, in fact, the observer of your mind and the perceiver of your thoughts, and you can choose which thoughts to entertain and which thoughts to ignore.

A four-step process to overcome limiting beliefs

Step 1 - Identifying your limiting beliefs

In which areas of your life are you unhappy? Where are you being held back? Do you already have any negative beliefs?

Look at each area of your life one by one and ask yourself, "What are the real reasons I'm unsatisfied in this area?" If you consider the thoughts arise in response to this question, you'll be able to figure out what you're thinking and what stories you're telling yourself.

One thing I recommend you to do is to look at a wheel of life and figure out the area in which your biggest goal belongs—to find it online, simply google "wheel of life." How well is this area of your life going? Do you honestly believe you can achieve your goal? If not, what limiting beliefs are telling you you can't?

Some areas to consider:

- Career
- Family
- Finance
- Health
- Personal Growth
- Relationships
- Social Life

Now it's time to develop a better understanding of just how a limiting belief can affect you. Let's use, 'I'm not good enough,' a very common limiting belief, as our example. This belief causes the following side effects:

- **Procrastination.** You'll want to put things off and think along the lines of, "I'll do it later. I don't feel confident, and I would fail if I do it now."

- **Quitting.** You'll find yourself looking for reasons to give up and you'll want to quit at the smallest sign of failure, be it real or imagined. You'll say, "See! I told you I'm not good enough."
- **Self-sabotage.** To ensure your failure and validate your feelings of incompetence and worthlessness, you will set goals that are too big to be accomplished in too short a timeframe.

Realizing the constant warfare between you and your subconscious is half the battle. Having negative thoughts is normal, but you should *never* allow them to prevent you from moving forward. It's okay to acknowledge your negative thoughts, but you shouldn't accept them as if they were the ultimate truth.

Your mind might tell you repeatedly you aren't good enough, or you can't do this or that, but your thoughts and feelings are not who you are. You are the individual who observes these feelings. People often use "I am" statements when discussing their emotions, such as "I'm sad" or "I'm angry," but these words are misleading. We ourselves aren't sad or angry, we just *feel* sad or angry. It isn't our identity. Think of feelings as mental clouds passing through your mind. They'll disappear as soon as you accept them and let them go.

When you have negative thoughts, welcome them. Focus on your body and feel the way they manifest within you. Then, give yourself permission to let them go. Accepting you have an unwanted thought doesn't mean accepting it as true. It only means you welcome the thought, realize it doesn't define you, and make a conscious choice to discard it.

Step 2 - Befriending your subconscious mind

The second step is to identify the intention behind the limiting belief. Your subconscious mind is always trying to protect you. It does whatever it can to help you. However, it doesn't necessarily know what can truly help you. Don't fight it, instead, befriend it and collaborate with it. Can you identify the positive intention behind your limiting belief? How is your subconscious mind trying to help you?

Step 3 - Arguing with your subconscious mind

After befriending your subconscious mind, the third step involves arguing with it.

Ask yourself the following question: Is this limiting belief true all the time in every possible situation? Then, look for evidence showing you it isn't. To continue with our previous example, look for all possible evidence that you *are* good enough and you *can* achieve your goal. For instance, you can look at past successes.

Start arguing with your mind on a daily basis. When your mind says you aren't good enough, ask yourself what you *are* good enough to do. Asking this question on a daily basis allows you gradually to deconstruct the belief. If you keep focusing on what you're good enough to do, it will eventually become habitual and you'll begin seeing more and more things you do well.

Start small. The idea is to train your mind to focus on what makes you good enough. When you do this, your subconscious mind will learn to scan your environment for supporting evidence. Remember, if you focus on a thought long enough it will ultimately become a belief.

Examples:

- I'm good enough at cleaning my desk
- I'm good enough to make friends
- I'm good enough to learn a foreign language
- I'm good enough to study
- I'm good enough to exercise.

You can probably come up with thousands of reasons why you *are* good enough.

Gather written evidence

Start writing all your accomplishments in a journal. Or better yet, start writing every single thing you accomplish on a piece of paper and put each one in a jar. Then watch the jar fill up as the weeks pass. You'll notice there are countless things you can do well. There are also things you aren't so good at, but we all have challenges to overcome. Nobody's perfect. Does this mean you're not good enough? I would seriously challenge this assumption.

If you use the above method, eventually, you'll realize unworthiness is not part of your identity. You'll also realize it applies in very limited situations in your life, if any. It will soon become clear to you that you *are* good enough.

You don't have to stop there, however, you can repeat this process for each of your limiting beliefs. If "I'm too old to *insert your goal here*" is your limiting belief, you can gather examples of people who achieved amazing things in their seventies, eighties, nineties, or even hundreds. Fauna Singh ran a marathon at over 100-years-old! You can write your successes in a notebook and even add pictures.

Keep gathering evidence, and soon enough, you'll realize your belief is just that: a belief and not fact.

Step 4 - Replacing your limiting belief with a more empowering one

To create your new, empowering belief, all you have to do is look to its opposite. In the case of 'I'm not good enough,' you could replace it with 'I'm worthy.' You could further specify it to address your needs.

- I'm worthy of love.
- I'm worthy of success.
- I'm worthy of having an amazing girlfriend/boyfriend.
- I'm worthy of achieving *insert your goal here*.

Bonus step

Write a letter to your subconscious mind that you can read out loud whenever you're faced with limiting thoughts or feel like giving up. Your subconscious mind is always trying to help you, but it often does so in ways that are, in actuality, totally unhelpful. When you realize your subconscious has good intentions and begin working with it, however, it'll be much easier to deal with your limiting beliefs. Below is an example of the kind of letter you might want to write for this step:

Dear Subconscious Mind,

You're telling me I'm not good enough. I know your intentions are good and this is your way of protecting me. I'm very grateful, but you don't need to do it anymore. I want to let you know I actually am good enough. I fully deserve to achieve my goal, and I'm completely worthy of it. I can handle failures because they're getting me closer to my goal. I'm learning a lot from them and am actually excited about failing more in the future. After all, each failure brings me one step closer to reaching my goal. I'm asking you to trust supporting me in my journey towards the goal that means so much to me. Thanks for your support!

Key Lessons:

Many people fail to achieve their goals because of the mental blocks and limiting beliefs they hold. Follow these steps to overcome them:

1. Be aware of the ways in which your mind is trying to make you give up. Accept your unwanted thoughts, realize you are not these thoughts. Allow yourself to let go of them.
2. Befriend your subconscious mind and identify the positive intentions behind your limiting beliefs
3. Challenge your limiting beliefs on a daily basis by looking for evidence of their falseness. Be on the lookout for new examples of limiting beliefs and gather written evidence.
4. Replace your old beliefs with new, empowering ones and create a affirmations from them.

BONUS step: Write a letter to your subconscious mind and read it aloud regularly.

Action step

Go through the four-step process using the workbook (*Section III. 7a. Four-step process to overcome limiting beliefs*).

Creating the right mindset

> *Successful people are not supermen. Success does not*

> *require a super-intellect. Nor is there anything mystical about success. And success isn't based on luck. Successful people are just ordinary folks who have developed belief in themselves and what they do.*
>
> — David J. Schwartz, The Magic of Thinking Big.

Choosing thoughts that serve you well

I'm always surprised to see how many people complain incessantly and insist everything is wrong in the world. They're always saying the economy is bad, all the politicians are corrupt, and everything is unfair. Some people are always complaining about the things they have no control over. Yet, there is no rule saying we have to focus on negative things all the time, or worry over that which we can't change. **Overcoming worrying requires action, and you can't do anything useful if you have no control over a particular situation.** If you can't or aren't able to do anything about a situation, you shouldn't waste time thinking about it. Ever.

Who says you need to allow negative thoughts to dwell in your mind? The quality of your thoughts will determine the quality of your life and **you are responsible for what you allow into your mind.** Unfortunately, negative thoughts and criticisms have a stronger impact than positive thoughts and praise, which is why it's so important to spend more time focusing on our positive thoughts. Taking the time to fill your mind with positive thoughts will ultimately cause your mind to generate more of them.

Our thoughts are not reality; they are merely our *interpretation* of reality. Our interpretation can be positive or negative. If you don't like your current interpretation of reality, change it by focusing on what you want, and you should do this as often as possible.

If you set ambitious goals during the exercises in this book—and I hope you did—someone around you will probably tell you one or more of your goals are unrealistic. But, have you ever thought about what the phrase, 'It is not realistic' means? It really has no meaning because it's completely subjective. When someone refers to your goals as 'unrealistic,' they're really saying: "What you're trying to accomplish isn't in line with my reality. My current belief system doesn't allow me to see it as possible." Of course, their reality is *not* your reality. Obviously, if you set big goals without doing what it takes to accomplish them, nothing will happen. But it's a totally different story if you choose the right goals, break them down, plan carefully, maintain the right mindset, and consistently take action. Doing these things will help you realize that your goal *is* possible, no matter what it is. I'm not saying it will be easy or you're guaranteed to accomplish it, but it's definitely possible!

Turning into a full-blown optimist

The difference between an optimist and a pessimist is what they choose to focus on. The pessimist chooses to see the glass as half empty while the optimist chooses to see it as half full—even though the volume of water in the glass is the same! Some people may argue optimists are out of touch with reality, but that would be a gross misinterpretation of optimism. Being optimistic doesn't mean denying reality. It just means making a conscious choice to focus on the positive side of things. It also means acknowledging unpleasant aspects of reality but choosing not to dwell on them. There is no law forcing us to concentrate on things that make us miserable. Remember, our unconscious mind is constantly eavesdropping on our thoughts, and those thoughts create our reality.

Unfortunately, most people spend the bulk of their time worrying about useless things. This was illustrated well by Earl Nightingale, a famous motivational speaker who said the following:

> *Let me show you how much time we waste in worrying about the wrong problems. Here is a reliable estimate of things people worry about: Things that never happen 40%, things that are over and past and that can never be changed by all the worry in the world 30%, needless worries about our health 12%, petty miscellaneous worries 10%, really, legitimate worries 8%. In short, **92% of the average person's worries take up valuable time, cause painful stress even mental anguish, and are absolutely unnecessary.***

Are you worrying about useless things?

If you're prone to worry and have a difficult time being optimistic, these tips will help you become a genuinely optimistic person:

1. Stop watching so much TV.
2. Stop reading and watching the news or, at the very least, do so weekly instead of daily.
3. Never buy into other people's 'reality' or pessimism.
4. Stop hanging out with negative people. If that's not an option, seek to limit your time with them as much as possible.
5. Read, watch, or listen to motivational books or videos on a daily basis. I recommend Chicken Soup for the Soul by Jack Canfield, which contains many short but inspiring stories. You might also want to take a look at motivational videos on YouTube.
6. Train yourself to reframe all situations into opportunities or learning experiences, no matter how bad they are. This may sound difficult, but I assure you it's possible! You can

find something positive about any situation. It could be something as simple as making you stronger, or being proud of yourself, for working hard to maintain a great attitude in spite of your difficulties. What happens to you doesn't matter, but how you choose to react to it does.

Visualizing your way to success

> *Your nervous system cannot tell the difference between an imagined experience and a 'real' experience. In either case, it reacts automatically to information which you give to if from your forebrain. Your nervous system reacts appropriately to what 'you' think or imagine to be true.*
>
> — Maxwell Matlz, Psycho-Cybernetics.

When it comes to developing ourselves and improving our lives, imagination is one of the most powerful tools available. Our imagination allows us to create whatever experiences we want at any given time. You can enjoy various scenarios and situations in your mind as often as you want and at no monetary cost. In fact, professional athletes, chess players, army generals, CEOs, and other successful people use visualization on a daily basis. We all use visualization, even if unconsciously. However, if you're like most people, you're probably visualizing negative things. You might be worrying about the future and visualizing yourself losing your job or failing an exam. You might also be dwelling on past failures.

In reality, we can't clearly distinguish real experiences from "fake" ones, which means we can trick our minds by simulating desired experiences through visualization. The more details you visualize, the more your brain will interpret the experience as real. If you feel you lack imagination, don't worry, imagination is like a muscle, and visualization is a great opportunity to strengthen it.

In the 1960s, an experiment was conducted to evaluate students on their ability to make free throws in basketball under various conditions. Students were divided into three groups. The first group was asked to train twenty minutes a day for twenty days, a second was asked not to train at all, and the third was asked to imagine themselves making free throws twenty minutes a day for twenty days. Ultimately, the group of students who practiced only in their imagination performed almost as well as those who practiced in reality. Specifically, those who practiced improved their scores by 24% while those who practiced in their imaginations improved by 23%. Students who refrained from both visualization and physical training showed no improvement. This experiment has been replicated many times since and has continued to produce similar results.

More surprisingly, studies have shown it is possible to build strength and fuel weight loss just by using visualization techniques! One experiment sought to measure the increases in strength among three different groups of people. Those in the group who used audio CDs to visualize working out, improved their strength at a rate similar to those who actually worked out. At the end of the two-week experiment, the group that engaged in 'virtual' workouts improved their strength by 24%, while the group that carried out actual physical exercised improved by 28%!

Visualization is an effective way to influence your subconscious mind and mold it little by little. The more you visualize your goal, the more confident you'll feel about your ability to achieve it. Visualization will give you the motivation and the drive necessary to continue moving forward. It will also encourage your subconscious mind to focus on what you want rather than what you don't want. This will ultimately help you overcome your limiting beliefs and avoid self-sabotage.

As you continue to align yourself with your goal, you'll find yourself doing and trying things you wouldn't have dared to previously. For me, visualizing my goals has helped me take more action towards achieving them. It has also caused me to redefine continually what's possible for me.

Focusing on what you want is vital, so take a few minutes every morning to visualize your goals.

When you visualize, it's key to put yourself in a positive emotional state. Imagine how you'd feel if you had already accomplished your goal. Practice this on a daily basis. The more you can remain in such an empowering emotional state, the more resourceful you'll become. You'll feel more inspired, more creative, and more confident, which will cause you to take more action towards your goal.

Creating a vision board to supercharge your dream

> *We have to see ourselves there long before it happens.*
>
> — Eric Thomas, motivational speaker.

You might want to create a vision board. A vision board, or dream board as it's sometimes called, is a board where you gather all your goals. Use pictures to symbolize your goals, and allow you to visualize them all simultaneously. You could use a picture of a nice home to signify your dream house, a book to signify the novel you want to publish, or a happy couple to signify your ideal relationship. The possibilities are endless. Put your vision board in a place where you can see it every day. Keep in mind you can create a digital vision board to use as a wallpaper or screensaver on your computer.

Despite what movies like *The Secret* might tell you, a vision board alone won't allow you to magically achieve your goals. It will, however, help you focus on your goals and make them more concrete within your mind. This will ultimately influence your subconscious. The mind is very good at finding information pertinent to the things you tell it to focus on, but don't forget to couple your focus with action!

You might believe many things are out of your reach, but have you ever asked yourself *why* you hold this belief? Are they truly out of reach from an objective standpoint, or does your current, subjective reality make them seem this way?

When you start building a more positive mindset, work on overcoming your limiting beliefs, and visualize your goals as often as possible, you'll gradually create a new reality. As you close the gaps between your thoughts and your goals, you'll be doing more and more to make your dreams a reality. In the end, your thoughts will determine your actions and therefore your reality.

Key Lessons:

To achieve your goal, it's essential to create an empowering mindset. Below are a few ways you can do this.

1. **Choose thoughts that serve you:** Focus on empowering thoughts that keep you in a positive emotional state and encourage inspired action.
2. **Become a full-blown optimist:** Remove negativity from your life and focus on the positive side of things. Let go of all the petty worries you can't do anything about. Remember, 92% of your worries are useless.

3. **Visualize your goals:** Empower your subconscious mind by visualizing your goals repeatedly. Feel as though you've achieved your goals and practice moving through your day with confidence.

∽

Action step

Do the exercises in the workbook. (*Section III. 7b. Creating the right mindset.*)

∽

4

OTHER KEY CONSIDERATIONS

In this section, I'll cover some more issues that are crucial to consider when setting goals. I'll discuss topics like the pros and cons of sharing your goals, how to create accountability, the importance of being flexible with your goals, and whether or not to abandon them.

On Sharing Your Goals

Should you share your goals?

The decision to share your goals with others is a personal one, and you must consider the pros and cons before doing so. Let's start with the benefits. Sharing your goal might be an effective way to motivate and hold yourself accountable. Sharing your goals with colleagues, family, or friends shows commitment and makes it harder for you to give up.

It might also help you make goals that are realistic and have reasonable chances of being achieved. If you consistently fail to reach your goals, your self-esteem will suffer and those you've shared them with might mock you. For this reason, you'll have a strong incentive to think carefully about your goal and ensure your deadlines are reasonable.

As I alluded to earlier, when you share your goal, be sure to use words that show confidence. The words you use have a big impact on the way you feel, so this will help your goal become a part of your reality. I've found sharing my goals with many people doesn't just motivate me, it also opens me up to new opportunities. The more you share your passion and talk about your goals, the more likely you are to meet people who can help you achieve them. But again, clarity is important. If you know exactly what you want and are truly passionate about it, people won't just want to help you, some of them might also know how to do it.

Additional tip:

When you speak of your goals, try to avoid the following words:

- Would
- Could
- Should
- Might
- Try
- Hope
- Wish
- Maybe
- Perhaps.

Use this next set of words and phrases as much as possible:

- I will
- Absolutely

- Definitely
- Of course
- Surely
- Certainly
- Obviously
- Without a doubt
- No problem.

The downside to sharing your goals

Now we're going to discuss the disadvantages of sharing your goals. Below are four pitfalls to avoid when sharing your goals.

1. Setting your goals too low: One risk is you may end up setting your goals too low to avoid being ridiculed if you fail to achieve them..

2. Setting your goals too high: Another is setting them so high they are impossible to reach, which will erode your self-esteem and make it harder to trust yourself, if and when you fail.

3. Sticking to outdated or irrelevant goals for too long: You have to accept the fact, for various reasons, there will always be goals you don't achieve. If you commit yourself publicly to a specific goal, you might feel peer pressure to stick with it even when it's no longer important to you. This pressure might reinforce your 'why' so much, it lingers and becomes a burden, even after you've outgrown your goal. The pressure may be intense, but it shouldn't control you.

Let me give you an example from my own life. When I shared my goals on my website, I thought announcing them meant I had to accomplish all of them no matter what. As a result, I put a lot of pressure on myself and ultimately felt overwhelmed. Eventually, I realized it was impossible to accomplish everything on my list, and started refocusing on what truly mattered to me—working on my blog, researching, and writing this book.

Sharing your goals could have some negative consequences if you lose sight of what matters to you, so remember, your goals are supposed to support you. **Don't let peer pressure force you to stick to goals that have become irrelevant to you.**

4. Mistaking discussing your goals for working on them:

In one of his talks given during a TED conference, an event aiming at spreading valuable ideas all around the world, the American entrepreneur Derek Silvers explained that, according to recent studies, sharing your goals could make them less likely to happen.

When we share our goals, they tend to become part of our reality and feel almost as if they've been accomplished. This may give us instant gratification and superficially improve our present reality, but it doesn't move us closer to a successful outcome. On the contrary, this could undermine our desire to work hard to achieve them.

I believe talking about your goals can be useful if done properly, but it's important not to get too caught up in the dialogue. When you share your goals, remember to do it with the intent of building accountability, not as a way to feel good about yourself.

Things to consider when sharing goals

Sharing goals will only be useful if you take the time to think about the benefits you're trying to gain from doing it. To help you decide whether or not to share them, consider the following points:

Benefits- What kind of benefits do I hope to get from sharing my goals?

Environmental components

- **Peer pressure**- How much does peer pressure affect me? Is it likely to prevent me from dropping or modifying my goal if necessary? If yes, are the benefits of peer pressure greater than their drawbacks?
- **Support factors**- How supportive are the people with whom I want to share my goals?

Goal-related factors

- **Goal type**- Is my goal likely to change over time?
- **Goal size**- How big is my goal? - Do you have big long-term goals you know people around you will likely dismiss as "unrealistic"? If so, I recommend you break them down into short-term goals that will likely be seen reasonable before sharing.
- **Number of goals shared** - Am I sharing just one goal or a list of them? •When you share a list of goals, you feel less pressure to accomplish all of them, which makes it easier to modify the list as needed.

Remember, you can always keep a goal to yourself. I share a lot of my goals, but I keep some big ones to myself, or only share with very close friends.

Accountability partner & mastermind group

Having an accountability partner who can monitor your progress, provide motivation, and give advice might be the best way to share your goals. People hire life coaches for this very reason—they want to clarify their goals and have someone to support them in making the changes necessary to achieve them. If you want to share your goals, why not look for an accountability partner among your friends? You could even create a mastermind group, which consists of people who come together to discuss their respective goals and support each other.

When creating a mastermind group or looking for an accountability partner, make sure:

- All group members are positive people who support and believe in you. Choose people with whom you are comfortable. Avoid including negative friends. In a group like this, they will drag you down!
- You have a clear agreement from the very beginning to ensure you're all on the same page. It's advisable to make a rule that requires honest and constructive feedback, even if the feedback is not necessarily what the other person wants to hear. After all, a group that doesn't allow you to be honest with yourself and others, won't be of any use.
- All members are starting with similar levels of "success". You don't want someone to feel superior because their accomplishments are always bigger than everyone else's. Nor do you want someone to feel inferior because their accomplishments are always smaller than those of other group members.

Remember, a mastermind or accountability group should inspire and motivate both you and the other group members. It should also provide members with valuable advice and help them move forward. Though peer pressure and guilt can motivate people, it's a subpar incentive. If you find this occurring in your group, feel free to leave it. You shouldn't continue doing something that no longer serves you.

On Flexibility

Is it ever okay to abandon a goal?

If you are someone for whom keeping promises is paramount, or you tend to be stubborn once you've set your mind to something, abandoning a goal might seem unthinkable. Perhaps you feel it would hurt your pride to give up the goal, or you don't want to pass up the chance to prove yourself. Regardless, you should never lose sight of the fact goal setting is supposed to bring you closer to your dream life. It should help you achieve goals that excite you and are aligned with your life purpose and values. As personal development blogger Steve Pavlina wrote, *"If it doesn't improve your present reality, then the goal is pointless, and you may as well dump it."*

You also have to realize, as you read new books, acquire new knowledge, meet new people, and learn more about yourself, your values may change. You may need to fine-tune your life purpose as a result.

If you realize a goal is no longer relevant, exciting, or deeply connected with your values and life purpose, don't hesitate to let it go. You aren't here to live up to other people's expectations, you don't have to prove anything to anyone, and you certainly shouldn't pursue a goal just because you've publicly committed to it.

A real-life example of flexibility

In August 2014, I created a list of goals I wished to achieve by the end of the year. As I was working towards these goals, I soon realized the list was too long. Some goals were no longer exciting, and others were actively unhelpful. Some were related to coaching, which is an area of huge interest for me. However, I became more excited about creating my blog and working on this book, both of which made sense to do before coaching. I didn't take long to realize I didn't have enough time to study coaching seriously, or coach enough people to make the experience worthwhile. I decided to postpone coaching until I would be able to do it in a way that was much more intensive and effective than I originally planned. I went through a similar experience regarding my goal of giving a seminar on personal development by the end of the year. In a more general sense, I became intensely aware of the need to spend a considerable amount of time marketing my blog, if I wanted to increase traffic. For these reasons, I refocused my efforts on my blog and postponed my other goals.

Remember, your goals should always guide you towards the life you dream of.

When stubbornness goes wrong

A certain degree of stubbornness is essential when it comes to attaining your goals, but too much can be a hindrance. Take the following example from my own life: While majoring in Japanese, my friend and I decided to challenge ourselves to take and pass level 2 of the Japanese Language Proficiency Test. We would have a year to prepare, but had only been studying Japanese for a few months at the time. As such, the test would be difficult, and we would have to spend a year studying for hours and hours each day to have a chance at passing it. My friend quickly realized this goal was not yet worthy of pursuing. He figured, quite reasonably, he could take the exam in two years rather than one. I, however, decided to go for it, and ended up spending several hours a day studying. I ultimately passed the exam, but I can't say it was worth it. I eventually wondered why I didn't wait longer to take the exam. If I had, I wouldn't have had to study as hard. Challenging ourselves is great but we need to do it for the right reasons. I was simply trying to prove I could accomplish my goal and keep my promises. In truth, the goal wasn't helping me improve my present reality, nor was it an efficient use of my time. The major take away from this story is: **goals are supposed to help you, not waste your time!**

Should I adjust my goal over time?

While working on your goals, you may come up with new ideas and encounter new perspectives or opportunities. As a result, your original goal is likely to change over time. When this happens, take the time to work out whether the new opportunity or idea is truly exciting to you. Next, ask yourself why you want to pursue the new opportunity and figure out if these reasons outweigh the desire to stick to your original plan.

When something new arises, the people around you might tell you to seize the golden opportunity. You might even rationalize it's your best option because you'll earn more money, gain more stability, or earn more recognition. If your friends were you, they would go for it. The thing is, they aren't you, and you are striving to achieve *your* goal, not theirs. When deciding whether or not to go a certain way, ask yourself, "Does it make *me* feel good?" If money, stability, or recognition are not priorities for you, you won't have the motivation to pursue a goal that offers them—because they won't really inspire you.

It's easy to forget how important it is to follow our emotions or gut feelings when making decisions in life. **Don't let social pressure dictate the goals you strive to achieve.** Listen to your emotions and adjust your goals when you feel the need.

On visualization

What if I can't visualize?

You may be thinking, "I try to visualize, but I can't." We all visualize differently. Some can see clearer pictures than others, but it doesn't matter in the end. Just think of yourself as having already accomplished your goal, whatever that may mean to you. Don't overthink it. The idea is to put yourself in a positive emotional state, one that gives you the confidence, creativity, courage, and motivation to keep working on your goal every day.

CONCLUSION

Thank you again for purchasing and reading this book. I hope it has been of help.

Setting goals is one of the best decisions you will ever make. By deciding to set clear goals, you've made the decision to take full responsibility for your life and start creating the life you truly deserve.

My sincere hope is that this book leads you to think about your life, clarify your values, and determine the direction in which you want to go. If you follow the methods outlined within these pages, you'll achieve all the goals that really matter to you and overcome the challenges you'll encounter on the road to attaining them.

I encourage you to refer to this book as often as necessary. Use it as a motivator and a tool to achieve your goals. Remember: your goals are supposed to support you. Use them as a source of inspiration and they will take you as far as you want to go, but only if you have a clear plan and take action consistently.

You will likely fail many times while setting goals. You may set long-term goals, but fail to set daily or weekly goals consistently. You may give up setting short-term goals before starting again a few months later. You may set daily goals at work while giving yourself more freedom and spontaneity in your personal life. You may end up creating your own personal goal setting method, or you may simply set a general direction while allowing yourself great flexibility. These are all fine. In the end, what matters is:

- Do your goals help you achieve a higher level of fulfillment in your life?
- Will you regret not achieving certain goals?

You've reached the end of this book so, I'm guessing you must really like it. I appreciate you reading this far! You know, as a self-published author, it is often really tough to market my book the way the big publishing houses can. So, if you could take a few minutes to leave an honest review I would really appreciate it.

Thanks so much for your support! I look forward to hearing from you very soon. Join me on Facebook by searching for:

whatispersonaldevelopment.org

Many thanks! May your goals take you to where you deserve to be.

Thibaut Meurisse

Founder of whatispersonaldevelopment.org

What do you think ?

I want to hear from you! Your thoughts and comments are important to me. If you enjoyed this book or found it useful **I'd be very grateful if you'd post a short review on Amazon.** Your support really does make a difference. I read all the reviews personally so that I can get your feedback and make this book even better.

Thanks again for your support!

Bibliography

Books:

Goals

- *The Jim John Guide to Goal Setting*, Jim Rohn
- *The Magic of Thinking Big*, David Schwartz, PhD
- *The One Thing, The Surprisingly Simple Truth Behind Extraordinary Results*, Gary Keller
- *Focal Point, A Proven System to Simply Your Life, Double Your Productivity, and Achieve All Your Goals,* Brian Tracy

Mastery

- *Talents is Overrated: What Really Separates World-Class Performers from Everybody Else*, Geoff Colvin

Habits

- *Habits That Stick: The Ultimate Guide to Building Powerful Habits that Stick Once and for All,* Thibaut Meurisse
- *Mini Habits: Smaller Habits, Bigger Results*, Stephen Guise
- *The Compound Effect*, Darren Hardy
- *The Willpower Instinct: How Self-Control Works, Why It Matters, and What You Can Do to Get More of It*, Kelly McGonigal PhD

Other

- *Secrets of the Millionaire Mind: Mastering the Inner Game of Wealth*, T. Harv Ecker

- *The 4-hour Workweek: Escape 9-5, Live Anywhere, and Join the New Rich*, Timothy Ferris
- *The Effective Executive*, Peter F. Drucker
- *The Sedona Method, Your Key to Lasting Happiness, Success, Peace, and Emotional Well-being*, Hale Dwoskin

Youtube videos:

Type the titles of the following videos in the YouTube search bar

- *Assumption of Your Desire*, Joseph Clough
- *Finding Your Sweet Spot to Achieve Goals*, Joseph Clough
- *Goal Setting Workshop*, Jim Rohn, host by Jeff Fire, Millionaire Team
- *How to Set Extremely Effective Goals*, Actualized.org
- *How to Set Goals: The Ultimate Step-By-Step Goal Setting Workshop*, Project Life Mastery
- *Keep Your Goals to Yourself*, Derek Sivers
- *Small Steps Create Big Leaps*, Joseph Clough
- *Super Charge Your Goals*, Joseph Clough
- *Your Depths of Visions*, Joseph Clough

Resources on Life Purpose:

How to Discover Your Life Purpose, Celestine Chua (Free ebook):

http://personalexcellence.co/free-ebooks/

The Meaning of Life: Discover Your Life Purpose, Steve Pavlina (article):

www.stevepavlina.com/blog/2005/06/the-meaning-of-life-discover-your-purpose

How to Discover Your Life Purpose in About 20 Minutes, Steve Pavlina (article):

www.stevepavlina.com/blog/2005/01/how-to-discover-your-life-purpose-in-about-20-minutes

OTHER BOOKS BY THE AUTHORS:

The One Goal: Master the Art of Goal Setting, Win Your Inner Battles, and Achieve Exceptional Results (Free Workbook Included)

Habits That Stick: The Ultimate Guide to Building Habits That Stick Once and For All (Free Workbook Included)

Wake Up Call: How To Take Control Of Your Morning And Transform Your Life (Free Workbook Included)

Productivity Beast: An Unconventional Guide to Getting Things Done (Free Workbook Included)

The Thriving Introvert: Embrace the Gift of Introversion and Live the Life You Were Meant to Live

ABOUT THE AUTHOR

THIBAUT MEURISSE

Thibaut Meurisse is a personal development blogger, author, and founder of whatispersonaldevelopment.org.

He has been featured on major personal development websites such as Lifehack, Goalcast, TinyBuddha, Addicted2Success, MotivationGrid or PickTheBrain.

Obsessed with self-improvement and fascinated by the power of the brain, his personal mission is to help people realize their full potential and reach higher levels of fulfillment and consciousness.

In love with foreign languages, he is French, writes in English, and has been living in Japan for the past 7 years.

Learn more about Thibaut at:

amazon.com/author/thibautmeurisse

whatispersonaldevelopment.org

thibaut.meurisse@gmail.com

Need some help to achieve your goals?

Hire me as a coach and I will help you achieve your goals.

More specifically we will work together to help you:

- Change your mindset and your habits
- Overcome limiting beliefs that are holding you back
- Build stronger self-esteem so that you believe in yourself and in your ability to achieve your goals
- Create an action plan and take consistent action towards your goals
- Discover your life purpose
- Stay on track with your goals long-term

To learn more contact me at thibaut.meurisse@gmail.com

Looking forward to hearing from you soon.

Thibaut Meurisse

WAKE UP CALL - PREVIEW

I. WHY EVERYBODY SHOULD HAVE A MORNING RITUAL

Taking control of your morning

What is the first thing you did this morning? Did you hit the snooze button of your alarm clock? Did you complain about the weather? Did you drink your coffee hoping that it would give you an extra boost to start your day?

Unfortunately, too many people are reactive. By this I mean that they go through life reacting to the things that go on around them often feeling powerless as a result of external circumstances. It is this attitude of powerlessness that starts their morning. They read the newspaper, which tells them how bad the economy is, how violent the world is, and how prevalent terrorism is. They don't choose their attitude, they don't choose their mood, and they don't set clear intentions for the day. They let everything from the people around them to the things they watch on television control them instead.

Regardless of your environment, the reality is that you have an incredible power to create and shape the world around you. This control starts in your mind. It always does. If you aren't priming your mind for positivity each day, you miss out on extraordinary opportunities for growth and self-actualization. In this book, we'll work on creating a morning ritual that creates sincere excitement and will, upon becoming a daily habit, have a major impact in all areas of your life. We'll work together to make sure it fully meets your needs.

Are you living up to your potential?

Most people will never reach even a fraction of their full potential. They'll remain a mere shadow of what they could have been, because they never make the conscious choice to create the life they want. They never sit down to write down what exactly they want in life. They never set clear intentions for their days. As Jim Rohn beautifully said "I find it fascinating that most people plan their vacations with better care than their lives. Perhaps that is because escape is easier than change."

I love this quote. Indeed, we may spend weeks or even months preparing for a vacation, be it within our country or overseas, but how much time are we really taking each year to craft our life plans? I don't know about you, but for most of us, we don't devote that much time to this.

I suspect that this has a lot to with the idea that we don't have the power to transform our lives. Unfortunately, this is a core belief that many of us have. It's something we may have been told by our parents or teachers. Or perhaps society conditioned us to believe that we have to accept things as they are and can't have what we want deep down inside. Most of us are products of our environment. If everybody around us feels powerless during our formative years, we end up feeling the same.

It never ceases to amaze me how powerless many people feel in their lives. I ran into a prime example of this recently when a 26-year-old woman earning an average salary revealed she was convinced that there was no way she could increase her earnings at any point in her life. Needless to say, she didn't believe in personal development.

I was drinking with some of my colleagues a few weeks ago when one of them mentioned that he didn't believe in personal development. That was difficult for me to understand. If you don't believe you have any sort of power to shape your life and go in the direction you want to go, what's the point? If you think it's pointless to improve yourself and condition your mind to adopt new, positive habits, how can you expect to get anywhere in life? A lot of people seem to feel stuck where they are and see no possibilities for a better future. I don't think anyone can be truly happy living with that outlook.

In a similar vein, many people in Japan don't believe that they can become fluent in another language because they "aren't good at foreign languages". As a result, they think I must be some kind of genius to be able to speak Japanese so well. Yet if you consider the fact that I've spent 10,000, if not 20,000 hours studying Japanese and have lived in Japan for many years, my ability to speak the language isn't impressive.

Your daily habits will determine who you become

It's what you do each day that determines your long-term results in life. You are, quite literally, what you do and think on a daily basis. As such, adopting a few simple daily habits can have a profound impact on the amount of success and fulfillment you experience in your life. This is something that we'll continue to see throughout this book. If you look at the people that most of us consider successful, they usually aren't geniuses. They aren't fundamentally different from you. The only difference between you and them is their daily thoughts and actions, or rather their daily habits regarding what they do, what they think, and what they choose to focus on. You can develop these same daily habits to support your personal goals and dreams.

The power of focus

Let me start by asking the following question: What do you think about most of the time? Where is your focus during the day? We have thousands of thoughts every day, but we're largely creatures of habits. Did you know that, for the most part, over 90% of the thoughts you have today are the same as the ones you had yesterday, the day before yesterday, last month, last year, or perhaps even several years ago?

The truth is, everyone has their own set of thought patterns. Yet there's one thing that all of our respective thought patterns share: They lead to a series of similar situations that continually repeat themselves. That's why some people find themselves facing the exact same relationship issues regardless of who their partner is. Do you find yourself attracting the same type of person every time you get into a relationship? If so, you're experiencing another example of the repetitive experiences our thought patterns may cause. Another example of this phenomenon is quitting a job you dislike for a new one you think you'll love, only to realize within a few months that both jobs are more or less the same.

We also go through repetitive phases. We eat healthy for a while, have a binge, return to eating healthy, and then do it all over again in a never-ending cycle. Understanding what you're thinking and why is important. In the last part of the book we'll touch on thought patterns and limiting beliefs. We'll discuss how you can identify them and what you can do to overcome them.

Our brains share the same fundamental characteristics, and they have a fondness for running on autopilot. As a result, it's crucial to make a conscious choice to control your thoughts and focus towards what you want to attract in your life. If you don't, you'll continue having the same unhelpful thoughts you've had for years, will keep falling into the same behavioral patterns, and will never be able to bring about the changes you want most in life.

As self-improvement expert Brian Tracy says, you become what you think about most of the time. He is one of many personal development experts who espouse this belief. If your thoughts control who you'll become and what kind of life you'll have, then learning to focus on what you want to do, be, and experience is one of the most important habits you can develop.

In that regard, my morning ritual has become a very effective way to focus my thoughts, stay on track with my goals, and remind me of my overall vision. I hope yours will allow you to do the same. We'll work together on creating a morning ritual that allows you to focus on what truly matters to you.

How I learned about morning rituals

I first heard about morning rituals from renowned motivational speaker Tony Robbins while watching some of his YouTube videos. These videos sparked my interest in incorporating a morning ritual into my own life. Since then, I got interested in implementing a morning ritual in my life. Despite my interest, however, I continually failed in my attempts to create a morning ritual. I tried Tony's program that was available on YouTube, but gave up after a few weeks. I also tried to wake up at 5 am each day because it was "what successful people do". I failed countless times at that one, too.

I knew that having a daily morning ritual would make a real difference in my life, but I just couldn't make it stick. Looking back, I can think of several reasons why I failed each attempt.

The first reason was a lack of genuine, long-term commitment. I didn't fully commit to creating a morning ritual because I didn't take it seriously enough. For instance, I could have committed to a 30-day challenge, but for some reason I didn't.

The second reason is that my morning ritual was an example of too much, too fast, too soon. In other words, it was overly ambitious. Considering I didn't have any previous experience with morning rituals, devoting an hour a day to it was beyond what I could handle at the time. Added to the fact that I was trying to wake up way earlier than what I was used to, it was a recipe for failure.

The third reason is that I had nobody to support me and to hold me accountable during the process. Interestingly enough, I had a friend at the time who was experimenting with Tony Robbins' "Hour of Power" series, but we just weren't keeping each other accountable. We both had great goals and good intentions, but guess what? He failed, too.

How I successfully created a morning ritual

It wasn't until the summer of 2016 that I finally managed to successfully adopt a daily morning ritual. You might be wondering how I did that considering the plethora of failed attempts behind me. Well, it was simpler than you might think.

Long story short, I invested in a program that focused on morning rituals, then made a firm commitment to stick with it. I ultimately realized that the primary reason I failed in the past was because I wasn't committed enough in the first place. To this end, I discovered that investing money in a program created a sense of dedication and the desire to take on a new habit no matter what.

I assume you want the same kind of push I did, and that this fueled your decision to purchase this book. I'd like to take the time to congratulate you for making that decision. You've taken the first step!

Once I started to think of my morning ritual as something that would benefit me for the rest of my life, great things started to happen. I'm now happy to say that since making that commitment to my morning ritual, I've been sticking to it each and every day, apart from a few exceptions that I'll cover later in the book. Now, it's your turn! Join me and experience the benefits a good morning ritual offers.

Learn more at amazon.com/author/thibautmeurisse

STEP-BY-STEP WORKBOOK

1. WHY GOAL SETTING IS IMPORTANT

I. Your expectations

Write a short statement below explaining why you want to set goals and what you want to get out of this book

To get a clearer direction/motivation. To be going toward something. To better understand what I need to have clearer goals.

2. HOW TO SET EXCITING GOALS

In this section we're going to shed the light on some of the pitfalls you've encountered as you set goals. Answer the following question. Don't worry about giving the perfect answers. These questions are here to help you figure out the problems you face when setting goals.

1. How to choose the right goal

a. Setting worthy goals

Rate yourself on a scale of 0 to 10 for the following things:

1. My current goals reflect my deeper values

0 _____ 10

2. My current goals excite me and energize me

0 _____ 10

3. I enjoy the process of working on my goals

0 _____ 10

4. My current goals are a way for me to give (love, support, value, hope etc.)

0 _____ 10

b. Avoiding pitfalls

Rate yourself on a scale of 0 to 10 for the following things:

1. I'm unaware of limiting factors

0 _____ 10

2. I'm excessively focused on my goal(s)

0 _____ 10

3. I'm feeling overwhelmed because of the size of my goal

0 _____ 10

4. I constantly want more and more and forget to enjoy the now

0 _____ 10

5. I'm overly focused on achieving specific numbers neglecting to focus on the process that will lead to my goals

0 _____ 10

6. I have too many goals and fail to achieve many of them

0 _____ 10

7. I jump from one opportunity to another, one course to another, not sticking long enough to a specific goal to achieve it

0 _____ 10

2. How to Set Inspiring Goals

A Powerful Goal Setting Exercise

a. What do I really want?

It's now time to set exciting goals. Write all the goals you really want to achieve no matter how crazy they might sound. Don't worry you don't need to share them with anybody. Make sure you cover all the areas in your life (relationship, health, career, finance…). Write as many goals as you can.

-

-

-

-

-

-

-

-

-

-

-

-

-

-

-

b. How am I going to get there?

What would the best version of yourself do to achieve these goals?

Choose your most important goal and come up with as many ideas as possible to achieve that goal.

c. What is my first step?

What is one tiny step that if taken today would get me closer to my goal?

My first step:

3. How to align your goal with your values

What would achieving my goal get me?

Identify the values behind your goal. The more you elaborate, the stronger you "why" will become, and the more realistic achieving your goal will become.

Write down what your goal will get you using the example below:

Goal: having a successful blog that generates 100,000 page views per month

Fulfillment as a result of helping people

- Happiness

- Enhanced Self-Esteem

- Stronger sense of purpose

A passive income

- More freedom

- Self-employment/independence

- An end to my daily commute

- The means of doing what I love

- The means to decide my own schedule

Extra time to:

- Write more books and articles
- Study coaching, hypnosis or psychology
- Improve my public speaking skills
- Start new, exciting projects

Better health

- The ability to take a rest when I need to, and
- Less stress as a result of loving what I do.

What my goal will get me:

4. How to align your goal with your life purpose

a. Discovering my life purpose (optional)

Complete some or all of the three exercises below:

Exercise 1: Finding the values behind my goal

Take the most important goal that you identified during the goal setting exercise and look at the values behind that goal? Take some time to think about those values and try to connect them with a possible life purpose.

What are possible core values behind my goal?

-

-

-

-

Exercise 2: Asking myself insightful questions

Do some self-introspection by asking yourself the following questions:

1. If I had all the money and time in the world what would I do?

2. What do I love so much that I'd pay to do it?
-

-

-

3. How can I get paid to do what I love to do?

4. Who do I envy?

Exercise 3: Writing down to tears my life purpose

Take a pen and a piece of paper or use the blank space at the end of this workbook and answer the following question: "What is my life purpose?" Don't overthink it; just write whatever comes to mind. Keep doing it until the sentence you write makes you cry.

This exercise is originally from Steve Pavlina's article, *How to Discover Your Life Purpose in About 20 Minutes*

3. SETTING SMARTEST GOALS

1. Making your goal specific (S)

a. The power of clarity

Clarity is power. Do the following exercise to experience it by yourself.

Take 15 seconds to list as many white things as you can. Write they down if you like

-

-

-

-

-

-

-

-

-

-

Now take 15 seconds to list as many white things in your refrigerator as you can.

-

-

-

-

-

-

-

-

b. Clarifying your goal

How can you make your goal specific? Write your answer below:

2. Having measurable goals (M)

a. Measuring your goal

How will you measure your goals on a regular basis? Write down your goal below in such a way that it can be easily measurable:

My goal:

b. Setting your own KPI

Write down your own KPI(s) for your goal below:

My KPI(s):

3. Setting goals that are achievable (A)

a. Setting realistic goals

Look at your current goal. On a scale of 0 to 10, how would you rate your ability to achieve it?

0 _____ 10

Ideally you want your answer to be a 7 or a 8. Of course, this is purely subjective, but your belief in your goal will greatly determine your ability to achieve it. Remember that, borrowing the worlds of Jack Canfield, there is no unrealistic goals, only unrealistic deadlines.

b. Chunking down your goal

How can you chunk your down into smaller manageable tasks? Write down your monthly goals, i.e, what you want to accomplish in the next 30 days that would move you closer to your goal. Then, do the same for weekly goals and daily goals.

What I want to accomplish this month:

What I want to accomplish this week:

What I want to accomplish tomorrow:

4. Having a clear deadline for your goal (T)

Write the deadline for your goal below:

5. Having an emotionally sustainable goal (E)

a. Identify the obstacles

What are all the possible obstacles I am likely to encounter and how will I overcome those hurdles?

b. Imagining the worse

What are the worse case scenarios? Spend some time to think about them and prepare yourself mentally

Worse case scenarios:

c. Innoculing yourself against failure

To be able to persevere in the face of future setbacks take the time to answer the following questions:

How do I perceive failure?

What could I do to change that perception?

What am I willing to go through before giving up?

-

-

-

-

-

-

d. Reconnecting with your why

Write down the why behind your goals. What does your goal matter, and how will you remain motivated during tough times.

My Why:

-

-

-

-

-

-

e. Dealing with self-criticism the right way

What do you want your inner talk to be as you work towards your goals? Imagine being your own coach, best friend, lover and biggest fan

Me (coach):

Me (best friend):

Me (Lover):

Me (biggest fan):

f. Avoiding Planning pitfalls

Add an extra buffer to your original deadline:

My new deadline:

6. Strategizing your goal (S)

a. Understanding the rule of success

Do I know everything I should know to reach my goal? Yes No

What step I am going to take to get the information I need:

a1. Filling the gap

What specific skill(s) do I need to develop in order to achieve my goal?

-

-

-

a2. Using the 80/20 Rule

Answer the two questions below to make sure that you're using your time productively.

What are the key tasks on which you should focus your efforts?

-

-

-

-

What are the tasks that, while disguised as work, are more a distraction than pure work?

-

-

-

-

a3. Learning new skills with deliberate practice

What is the best way for me to master the skills needed to reach my goal?

a4. Leveraging the power of daily habits

Answer the following questions:

What are 3 steps I can take every day to get closer to my goal?

-

-

-

How can I turn my tasks into daily habits?

Every day I will:

-

-

-

-

a5. Investing in your goals

Answer the following questions before deciding to invest in a course

- How reliable is the program I am interested in?
- How much time can I save by buying this program/How much do I value an hour of my time?
- How much money can I make or save in the long-term by using that program?
- In what extent will I avoid distraction by buying that program?
- What are other potential benefits (peace of mind, commitment to take action…)

b. Scheduling for success

Planning your month like a pro

Write down three to five goal-related project or tasks you want to complete this month:

Task #1:

Task #2:

Task #3:

Task #4:

Task #5:

Planning your week like a pro

Write down three to five goal-related project or tasks you want to complete this month:

Task #1:

Task #2:

Task #3:

Task #4:

Task #5:

Planning your day like a pro

Write down three to five tasks you want to complete tomorrow:

Task #1:

Task #2:

Task #3:

Task #4:

Task #5:

7. Transferring your goal to the subconscious (T)

a. Four-step process to overcome limiting beliefs

Step 1 - Identifying limiting beliefs

For this exercise, identify one limiting belief in one area of your life. Ask yourself, what is holding me back in that area?

Some areas to consider

- Career
- Family
- Finance
- Health
- Personal Growth
- Relationships
- Social Life

My limiting belief:

Step 2 - Befriending your subconscious mind

Identify the intention by that limiting belief. How is your mind trying to protect you? Write your answer below:

Step 3 - Arguing with your subconscious mind

Argue with your mind, find evidence that your belief is not true. Use the blank space below to write down counter-examples from your past experiences, from different areas of your life or from other people (feel free to use a journal instead)

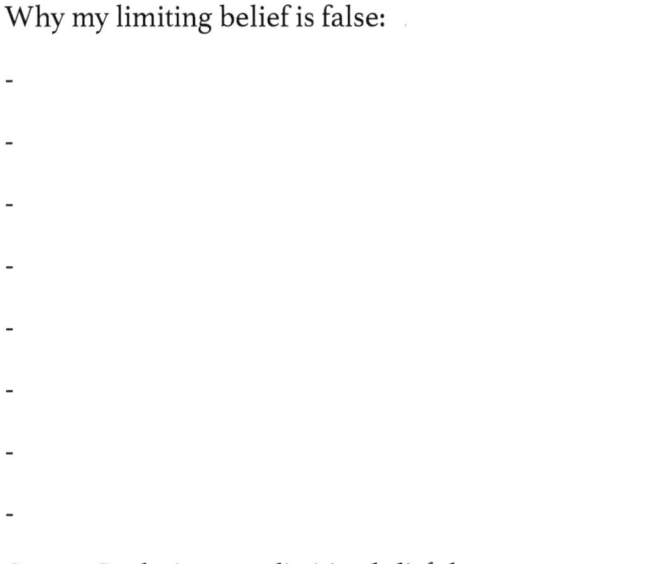

Why my limiting belief is false:

-

-

-

-

-

-

-

-

Step 4 - Replacing your limiting beliefs by a new empowering one

Create a new empowering belief that you want to implement in your life (usually the opposite of your current belief)

My new empowering belief:

Turn your new empowering belief into a compelling affirmation.

My positive affirmation:

*Make sure you spend some time reading out loud or writing down your new affirmation several times in the morning and/or in the evening.

Bonus Step: write a letter to your subconscious mind

Use the free space at the end of this workbook or a separate sheet of paper to write a personal to your subconscious mind.

b. Creating the right mindset

Turning into a full-blown optimist

What action will you take on a regular basis to become more optimist? Some ideas below:

1. Reduce the time I spend watching TV.
2. Stop reading/watching the news or do so weekly instead of daily.
3. Never buy into other people's "reality" or pessimism.
4. Stop hanging out with negative people.
5. Read, watch, listen to motivational books, or videos on a daily basis.
6. Train yourself to reframe all situations into opportunities or learning experiences, no matter how bad they are.

Action(s) I will take:

c. Visualizing your way to success

Visualize yourself as having already achieved your goal. How would you feel? Practice putting yourself in that positive emotional state every day. You'll feel more confident and be more motivated to work on your goal. It will also help you be more creative.

d. Creating a vision board to supercharge your vision

Choose one of the options below:

1. Create a physical vision board
2. Create a digital vision board on your computer (powerpoint slides, wallpaper, Evernote etc.)
3. Create a goal journal in which you write your goals and add pictures

2 Powerful questions to ask yourself every day

- If I could only accomplish one task today, what is the task that would have the most impact? What about this week? This month?
- If I keep doing what I've done today, am I going to achieve my goal? Be honest with yourself!

2 Powerful questions to ask yourself on a regular basis

- How could I accomplish my goals in only 6 months? 3 months? 1 month? What about 1 week? (Assuming a

yearly goal). It is a great way to brainstorm and to motivate yourself to take more action. If you are taking actions that have little impact and consciously or unconsciously procrastinate, this question will put you back on the right track. It's a good idea to ask yourself that question every week when you plan your activities for the following week.
- Assuming I failed to reach my goal, what would be the reason

Printed in Poland
by Amazon Fulfillment
Poland Sp. z o.o., Wrocław